CONSTANTINOPLE
In the Age of Justinian

— METE MALCIOĞLU
271- 7854

The Centers of Civilization Series

CONSTANTINOPLE

In the Age of Justinian

By Glanville Downey

NORMAN: UNIVERSITY OF OKLAHOMA PRESS

TO

MR. AND MRS. ROBERT WOODS BLISS
fautoribus et cultoribus bonorum

Library of Congress Catalog Card Number: 60–13473

Copyright © 1960 by the University of Oklahoma Press,
Publishing Division of the University.
Manufactured in the U.S.A.
First edition, 1960;
second printing, 1968; third printing, 1980.

PREFACE

THIS BOOK has been written to provide for the nonspecialist reader a picture of Constantinople as the center of the Byzantine Empire during the reign of Justinian, A.D. 527–565. In accordance with the purpose of the series of which it forms a part, the account is intended to show how, at a particular period, the city had been the setting for the development of a new synthesis of culture, which radiated from it over the Græco-Roman world, and beyond. Out of the considerable material which is available, I have tried to construct a portrayal and an interpretation, based on the original sources and on the results of modern research, which I hope will show the significance of Constantinople in an epoch which is still not sufficiently familiar to the modern world. It is during Justinian's reign that the different elements that formed the civilization of Constantinople—and of the Empire—can be most clearly perceived, and it was during this age that the enduring characteristics of Byzantine culture were being shaped. This epoch, looking both backward to classical antiquity and forward to the Renaissance and the modern history of Europe and the Slavic states, has much to teach us today about the origins and antecedents of our own world.

It is significant that not all scholars are in agreement as to when "Byzantine history" begins—whether in the time of Constantine the Great, for example, or the reign of Justinian, or even later. Equally significant is the use of different terms to describe the period—Late Roman, East Roman, Byzantine. These variations are natural reflections of the continuity between Byzantium and the classical world of which the Byzantines themselves were so keenly aware, and in which they found such important elements of strength.

In a treatment which does not make use of illustration, an attempt to describe and discuss in detail the art and architecture of the period could only be ineffective, and it would be pointless for this study to compete with the excellent picture books and histories of art and architecture which are readily available. In these the reader will find a pictorial supplement and commentary on the account and the interpretation offered here.

A work of this kind inevitably profits from the labors of many others and I must here record my debt to the scholars whose works I have consulted, as well as to colleagues and students from whom I have learned much. The book has benefited from the generous permission of several publishers to quote translations. The passages from Paul the Silentiary (pp. 111, 112) are reproduced from the translation in W. R. Lethaby and H. Swainson, *The Church of Sancta Sophia*, by courteous permission of Macmillan and Co., Ltd. The Faith Press, Ltd., generously granted permission for use of passages (pp. 122, 124–26, 129) from *The Divine Liturgy of St. John Chrysostom: The Greek Text with a Rendering in English*, third edition. The Society for Promoting Christian Knowledge kindly permitted use of quotations (pp. 125, 128–31), from *The Orthodox Liturgy, Being the Divine Liturgy of S. John Chrysostom and S. Basil the Great*, published by the Society for the Fellowship of SS. Alban and Sergius. The map is adapted, with grateful acknowledge-

PREFACE

ment, from that printed in J. B. Bury, *History of the Later Roman Empire*, London, Macmillan and Co., Ltd., 1923, Vol. I, facing p. 67.

My sincere thanks go to three friends who have read the manuscript, Dr. J. Elliott Janney of Cleveland, Professor Hugh Graham of the University of New Mexico, and Mr. Marvin C. Ross of Washington. Their generous criticisms and suggestions have done much to improve the book.

CONTENTS

CONSTANTINOPLE
In the Age of Justinian

THE CITY IS FOUNDED

OF THE VISITORS who came to Constantinople in the reign of Justinian (A.D. 527–565), perhaps the most fortunate were those who made the journey by ship through the Sea of Marmara, for they would first see the city as it rose above the water on its triangular peninsula, and the mass of buildings and the skyline, seen across the water, was a view never to be forgotten. The people of the city themselves had a deep love for their waters, the Sea of Marmara, the Bosporus, and the Golden Horn, which surrounded Constantinople on three sides. When Procopius, at the command of the Emperor Justinian, wrote his panegyrical account of the buildings which the Emperor presented to the city of Constantinople, he took many occasions to speak of the way in which the city was beautified by the sea, which, he says, "surrounds Constantinople like a garland"; and everywhere in Procopius' description there is evident the care which was taken to improve and embellish the shores of the city and its suburbs.

It was in fact as a maritime colony that the site had first attracted settlers, almost twelve centuries before the time of Justinian. Byzantion, the colony planted by the Greeks on the Bosporus, had been built around the acropolis which rose at the tip of the projecting triangle of land which commanded the southern end of the passage. This hilly promontory offered an incomparable site. From it, commerce to and from the Euxine Sea—including the grain shipped

3

to Greece—could be controlled, and the harbor of the Golden Horn, the northern side of the triangle, was one of the finest anchorages in the ancient world. The old Greek Byzantion became the Roman city of Byzantium; and when the Emperor Constantine the Great (A.D. 306–337) determined to found a new capital of his Empire in the East, Byzantium was transformed into Constantinopolis, the City of Constantine, the Second Rome or New Rome. Writers sometimes called it "the ruling city." People often referred to it simply as The City.

The visitor sailing up the Sea of Marmara would have his first view of the southern shore of Constantinople, which ran for something over three miles between the land walls, at the west, and the tip of the promontory at the east. He would see the massive sea wall, broken by two small protected harbors. Above the wall rose houses and palaces, and beyond one saw the skyline of the city—domes of churches and monumental columns bearing statues. The skyline as one approached would resolve itself into a series of hills and valleys; for like the old Rome, the new one was built on hills—though there was a little difficulty in making the number seven. The acropolis on the promontory stood about one hundred forty feet almost directly above the sea. Elsewhere the land sloped back from the water more gradually. Each hill had a different shape and a different height; the highest of the points stood about two hundred thirty feet above the level of the water.

If his vessel sailed round the eastern promontory toward the celebrated harbor of the Golden Horn, the visitor would be carried past one of the most magnificent sights in the empire—the first hill, the old acropolis, on which stood the Great Palace, the Hippodrome, the Senate House, and the broad public square of the Augustæum with its column bearing a statue of the Emperor. Towering above everything else was the great Church of St. Sophia, its dome rising one hundred eighty feet above the ground. The palace, occupying the slope from the Augustæum down to the water, seemed to personify the magnificence of the sovereign who dwelt in it.

Passing the tip of the promontory, and leaving behind the sight of the woods and meadows which lined the Asiatic shore of the Bosporus in Justinian's time, the visitor's ship would turn west and sail into the Golden Horn, the narrow bay which ran along the northern side of the city. The harbor had taken its name from its shape, which had been likened to the horn of a stag. Its advantages were remarkable. Nearly four miles long, it was in most places about a third of a mile wide. Its greatest depth, in the center, was over one hundred feet. Lined by hills and set off from the Bosporus by a bend in its lower course, the Golden Horn was protected on all sides from the winds. Procopius, in his description of Constantinople, wrote that this bay was always calm: even in the winter, when the Sea of Marmara and the Bosporus were struck by high winds, the Horn was peaceful and ships could enter it without a pilot. This ample and safe anchorage for both warships and commercial vessels proved throughout the history of Constantinople to be one of the chief reasons for the city's prosperity and security.

With two sides of the peninsula surrounded by water, the third side, which formed the base of the triangle, was closed by the land walls which ran from the southern angle of the peninsula to a point half way along the Golden Horn. Protected on two sides by water and defended on the third side by the massive walls of Theodosius II, the city would have been virtually impossible to capture by assault. Theodosius' defenses were not a single wall, but a set of three parallel walls, each higher than the last. The inner wall, which was the highest, and the middle wall were strengthened by towers placed at intervals. In front of the outer wall was a moat, sixty to seventy feet wide and over thirty feet deep, which could be flooded. At intervals along the four mile course of the walls were a series of gates, some designed for ceremonial, others for military purposes. The inner wall was from forty to seventy feet in height at various points and from twelve to forty feet thick.

Having seen only so much of the city, in the brief tour which has been sketched, a visitor could understand why Constantinople had been chosen when an eastern capital of the empire was needed; for in addition to its rare combination of natural advantages for defense, it was a center of communications for the empire and the countries beyond, north and south, east and west, by land and sea. It lay at the point where the crossing between Europe and Asia was easiest and it controlled shipping between the Euxine Sea and the Aegean and the Mediterranean. Commercially, it was a central point to which both raw materials and finished goods could be brought from all over the world; and the merchants of Constantinople were in an excellent position to export their goods not only to the empire but beyond its boundaries. The city's value as a military center was comparable. It could receive communications directly and by the fastest routes from the eastern or the western divisions of the empire, and it was a central point from which orders or troops could be dispatched most efficiently and most directly to any part of the empire.

The need for such an eastern capital was by no means

a new development in the time of Constantine the Great. Constantine's task had been the continuation of the labors of the Emperors Aurelian (A.D. 270–275) and Diocletian (A.D. 284–305) to save the empire from the crisis through which it had been passing in the third century. A number of circumstances had worked together to bring the Roman state almost to collapse. Decline of manpower, decline of production and commerce, inflation, inability of the army to defend the boundaries, which extended from Britain and the Rhine and Danube to the Euphrates— all these, coming at a time when the power of Persia was revived and growing, had strained the Roman military and economic systems, which were not capable of the extra exertion required in a sudden crisis of such magnitude. In the middle of the third century a series of weak emperors, succeeding each other at brief intervals, had to deal with repeated invasions of Syria and Asia Minor by the energetic King Shapur of Persia.

In part this state of affairs had come about from the dependence of the empire upon a single man—the sovereign. The emperor, as emperor, could win much or lose much; and from this time on the history of the Roman state was often chiefly a reflection of the personality of the ruler. Each emperor—including Justinian—was inevitably the heir of his predecessors. In this sense the preparation for Justinian's reign began in part in the third century. After the great crisis of the 260's, when the Emperor Valerian was actually captured by the Persians and died a prisoner, it was the good fortune of the Roman people that men like Aurelian and Diocletian were able to take over the state. Aurelian arrested the decline, and Diocletian began the process of restoration which was continued by Constantine.

After the perils through which the empire had passed, people began to look to the ruler for protection. In some ways, a supreme autocratic authority was welcomed. Under Diocletian and Constantine, the army was strengthened and a determined effort was made to save the economy which was being strangled by inflation and shortages in production. The civil administration was overhauled completely. The chief reform—growing out of the problems which led to the foundation of Constantinople—was the institution of the Tetrarchy. Diocletian had perceived that the empire had become so large, and its needs so complex, that it could no longer be governed safely or effectively by one emperor. It was also obvious that the Greek East and the Roman West each needed constant attention. Moreover, the differences in civilization and outlook that had always characterized Greeks and Latins were becoming progressively more manifest. Diocletian's plan—itself a practical one—was the division of East and West between two senior emperors *(Augusti)*, each assisted by a junior *(Cæsar)* who would in due time, on the death or retirement of the *Augustus*, succeed him as emperor. These four rulers, the Tetrarchs, could, it was thought, save the empire; and Diocletian, who had chosen the East, did by incessant travels restore order and prosperity so far as was then possible. Though he built palaces at Thessalonica and Antioch, he chose as his capital the city of Nicomedia, at the head of a gulf opening east out of the Sea of Marmara.

For a time the Tetrarchy worked as well as anyone could have expected; but after the abdication of Diocletian (A.D. 305), rival ambitions resulted in a series of wars among the tetrarchs, as a result of which Constantine the Great emerged as sole emperor (A.D. 324).

Under the Tetrarchy, Nicomedia had served as capital

8

of the eastern division of the Empire. In the West, a major change had to take place. With the needs of its world so radically altered, Rome could no longer be the center of the government, as it once had been. Something more directly in touch both with the other parts of the West and with the East as well was obviously needed. Various cities (Trier, Aquileia, Milan) served at times as headquarters of the administration in the West, but it was Ravenna, the "city of the marshes" on the Adriatic coast, that came to be regarded as the permanent western capital. Rome retained its traditional dignity, but the north Italian city, just below the Alps, had obvious advantages. It was a sign of the changes going on in the Roman state that it was possible to abandon the ancient capital, which had for centuries been the symbol of the empire's greatness, and to try the merits of other cities as possible capitals.

Such was part of what lay behind Constantine's decision, in A.D. 324, to found Constantinople, on the site of Byzantium, as a new single capital of the empire. Constantine concluded that the imperial headquarters needed to be much closer to the eastern provinces than Milan, Aquileia, or even Sirmium, which had served for a time as headquarters. But this eastern capital, of course, had to be in such a place that it was in direct and ready communication with the West. The situation of Byzantium answered the requirements. Its geographical, topographical, and military advantages over Nicomedia were obvious. (It may be that Diocletian would have preferred the site of Byzantium if he had wished to build a new capital; in Nicomedia he could establish himself in a large city better prepared to receive his court than Byzantium.) Whether the decision to found a new capital, and the choice of the site, had been taking shape for some time in Constantine's mind, we cannot now determine. In any case he acted promptly. The final battle that made him sole emperor took place on September 18, 324, at Chrysopolis (modern Scutari), directly across the Bosporus from Byzantium; and it was on November 8 of the same year that the work of transforming Byzantium into Constantinople was begun with a ceremony of the consecration of the site. Rome would have to be abandoned but its position of prestige would be maintained. Its ancient Senate could continue to function, and the emperors would pay the old capital fitting signs of respect on great occasions of the state. Constantinople would be a second Rome.

But the changing needs of government and war, and the benefits to commerce, were not the only reason for the origin of Constantinople. Constantine's new city was to be a Christian city, a Christian capital of an empire that had been pagan. For so great a change as this, a new foundation was required. Obviously an old and famous pagan city, such as Nicomedia or Thessalonica or Antioch, with long pagan traditions and associations, could not serve. Nicomedia itself, for example, might be unacceptable because of its associations as Diocletian's capital. On the other hand Byzantium was small enough so that it could be absorbed and disappear beneath the splendor of the new capital.

Thus Constantinople, as a new Christian city, represented both an end and a beginning—the end of the pagan Roman Empire and the beginning of the Christian Roman Empire. In the ending of one development, and its absorption into another process, lay the roots of the Constantinople of Justinian.

Constantine's conversion to Christianity, and the triumph of his army under the sign of the God of the Christians—"In This Sign Conquer"—gave a new direction to the history of the Roman Empire and to the development of western civilization. Some details of the process are not clear—some modern historians have challenged the reality and sincerity of the Emperor's conversion and the purity of his motives—but it is certain in any case that the emergence of Christianity as a tolerated religion, and then as the official state religion, could mean nothing less than a turning point in the history of Europe.

Part of the reason for some modern skepticism concerning Constantine's conversion had stemmed from the fact that the Emperor, on becoming a Christian, did not at once do away with the pagan forms of worship which had come to be associated with the imperial office. The Roman emperor had come to be regarded as a quasi-divine being, officially deified after his death, and he had received a formalized worship which had played an essential part in the unification of the diverse national elements which the empire embraced within its wide boundaries. At the time of Constantine's conversion, Christians were by no means the majority in the empire, and in particular, many of the chief officers in the army and the government were pagans, and their prompt adherence to the new religion was not to be expected. It is no wonder that Constantine felt he must proceed cautiously. It would be injudicious, as well as impossible, to do away with paganism at once. It was a sufficiently radical change for the empire to find itself governed by a sovereign who, from having ruled under the protection of Apollo, had become a Christian. This fact alone presented a problem of political theory such as the empire had never faced. How was the Christian emperor to receive the homage—and hold the loyalty—of both his pagan and his Christian subjects? What was to be the relationship of Christians, both as a church and as individuals, with paganism? How were Christians, no longer a persecuted class, to stand in relation to pagan culture and pagan literature? What would be the future status of paganism itself?

These were truly formidable questions, and it is not surprising that Constantine did not attempt to find immediate answers to all of them. Paganism, obviously, could not be killed with one stroke. At the same time the Church discovered that it had questions of its own to face. Suddenly, almost without warning, the Church stood in a position of power and responsibility, forced to deal immediately with issues, which it had not had to settle so long as it lived by itself in an alien society. What would be the official relationship of the emperor and the Church? The answer to this question of Cæsar and God had to take into account the traditional theory upon which the Cæsar's rule of his pagan subjects was based. After that came the question of the Christian and pagan society. This was a question as old as Christianity itself; but would the old answers to it be sufficient now that Christians found themselves in a wholly new status? How would the new status affect the answer?

These were the questions before Constantine and his people when Constantinople was founded. The city was in fact founded in order to provide answers to some at least of the questions. But one thing was plain, and that was that however bright the new era promised to be, the era would not—certainly could not—come into being all at once. Constantinople was a symbol, and a mighty symbol, of the beginning, but the creation of the new Christian state was not to be completed promptly. It was, in fact, not until two hundred years later that the sovereign was found who could undertake to organize and proclaim the fulfilment of the process. And so it was that the Constantinople of Justinian was the completion of the Constantinople of Constantine. Constantine's city was a magnificent creation, as splendid an imperial capital as could then be built; but it was founded in a time of troubles and designed to lead a transformation which could only grow slowly; and in some ways it could do no more than provide the setting for the final achievement of the vision as Justinian saw it. But Justinian's work could not have been done without Constantine's beginning. So the city itself provided the focal point which would serve each of these two emperors as the symbol and embodiment of his concept of the empire.

I

THE CITY OF JUSTINIAN AND ITS PEOPLE

By Justinian's day the new capital planned by Constantine had grown into a true Christian city, filled with churches—some of them the most famous in the world—with monasteries and convents, and with hospitals, orphanages, and homes for old people maintained by the Church. Yet at the same time it was a true classical city, showing its Græco-Roman origin everywhere, in its plan, its buildings, and its monuments.

To return to our visitor: when he became familiar with the city, he would see how its development had centered about a series of forums built in Roman style which were linked together by great thoroughfares. The Augustæum of Justinian's day, on the original acropolis of Byzantium, represented what had been the chief market place of the Greeks and later the forum of Roman imperial days. With the expansion of the city westward on the peninsula, there had come, first, the Forum of Constantine, west of the Augustæum, then the other forums, west and south of that of Constantine, all connected with one another by main streets. Along with the forums, the walls of the city had progressively moved west. The pre-Constantinian circuit, running west of the Augustæum, had been replaced by Constantine's wall, which enclosed roughly half of the peninsula; and this again, when the city had grown beyond it, had been supplanted by the wall of Theodosius II, which represented the ultimate development of Constantinople.

In this way the city had followed the pattern of expansion and city planning which was typical of the major centers of the Græco-Roman world, and Constantinople would not seem unfamiliar to any visitor who knew Rome, Alexandria, Antioch, or any others of the empire's large cities.

The commonest point of departure for a visit of the city would be the Augustæum, for it was here that the visitor would be taken to see the heart of the capital—and the heart of the empire. The setting was classical. The Hippodrome and the public Bath of Zeuxippus, which stood near it, opening on the square, had been built by the Emperor Septimius Severus (A.D. 193–211). Constantine had embellished the bath with ancient statues brought from other cities in the empire. On another side of the square stood the Senate House, built by Justinian in classical style to replace an earlier building which had been burnt. Here the Senate of Constantinople, though its power had been curtailed, kept up the ceremonies of its ancient tradition.

At an angle to the Senate House stood the gate of the Great Palace. Constantine the Great had built his palace in his new city on the plan of the imperial residence which had been adopted for Diocletian's palace at Spalato, and for other palaces elsewhere—the square plan based on the Roman army's standard fortified camp. Succeeding emperors had enlarged the Palace of Constantinople, building south and east on the slopes of the promontory which ran down to the Bosporus and the Sea of Marmara. Brick substructures were built out from the hillside to provide new space.

By Justinian's day the palace had become a vast and complicated group of gardens and terraces on different levels, with detached summer pavilions, churches, reception halls, a private stadium, and an indoor riding school.

CONSTANTINOPLE

Beneath these were a complex of storerooms, kitchens, stables, and servants' quarters. On the finest site in the city, the palace was designed for the comfort of the imperial family and the court in the sometimes trying climate of Constantinople, which was damp in winter, hot and humid in summer. The brick and marble buildings of the palace exhibited all the styles of monumental architecture that had been favored from the fourth century to the sixth. Changes in fashion could be seen notably in the figured mosaic floors, with their variety of geometric and floral ornament and their scenes based on the repertory of classical art, in which one could trace the development from the somewhat florid manner of the time of Constantine to the somewhat less rich style of Justinian's day.

Opposite the palace, on the other side of the Augustæum, stood the Church of St. Sophia, the shrine of Christ the Holy Wisdom of God. Built by Justinian to take the place of two earlier churches of the same dedication erected successively by Constantine and Theodosius II, the new St. Sophia, with its bold and massive design, soared above everything around it, and with its majesty and authority it seemed the chief building of Constantinople, symbolizing the roots of the strength of "the God-guarded City," as its people called it. As the most important church in Constantinople, it was sometimes referred to simply as "the Great Church."

Between the palace and the church, in the center of the square, rose a tall column of cut stone bearing a bronze equestrian statue of the Emperor Justinian. This monument—again a motif established in the art of imperial Rome—joined with the Hippodrome, the palace and St. Sophia in showing the visitor the three mainsprings of life in the capital—church, emperor, and people.

THE CITY OF JUSTINIAN

From the Augustæum the visitor might start to walk along the *Mesê* or Middle Street, paved with heavy blocks of stone, which ran the length of the city from the Augustæum to the Golden Gate at the southern end of the land wall. Like the main streets and forums of many cities, this thoroughfare was flanked on both sides by covered colonnades of tall columns supporting a stone roof which provided shelter from sun and rain. Constantine had built the first section of the street, leading from the Augustæum to the Forum of Constantine, and had ornamented the porticoes with classical statues. The sidewalks were lined with shops, and merchants sometimes built booths between the columns. At intervals there were staircases leading to the roofs of the colonnades.

As the visitor explored this part of Constantinople he would see the typical sights of a Græco-Roman city which had also acquired a certain amount of oriental flavor. In the busiest parts of the city the streets were crowded with people and animals. The every-day dress of both men and women was the wool tunic, which was covered with a wool cloak in cold or wet weather. The women's tunics and cloaks were amply cut and reached to the ground. Women's headdress was a scarf wound about the head, descending to the shoulders; the cloaks had hoods which could be pulled up, concealing the wearer's head almost completely.

The tunics of the men varied in quality, cut, and length according to the station and means of the wearer. Workmen's tunics were short, reaching to just above the knee, like the soldier's uniform. Gentlemen wore longer and more ample garments, sometimes falling to the ankle. The toga was no longer worn save on ceremonial occasions. Children's clothes were replicas of those of their parents. Some people went barefoot. Those who wore footgear had

17

sandals, low shoes of cloth or leather, or sometimes low boots of military type, reaching to the calf.

In the narrow streets only small vehicles could pass, and burdens were usually transported by donkeys, camels, or porters. All these carried heavy loads; the porters were much employed, for it was often easier and cheaper to hire a man than to use an animal.

Sometimes the streets would be filled with flocks of animals being driven to market. Here and there in the main streets one would see ladies of rank riding in brightly painted wooden carriages drawn by mules in ornate harness. Officials and well-to-do people rode horseback; noblemen could be seen on their white horses with saddle cloths embroidered in gold. Peddlers cried their wares, carried on donkeys or on their own backs, and itinerant merchants went from house to house selling food.

The *Mesê* would take the visitor past the Prætorium, the headquarters of the prefect or governor of the city, then to the oval forum named for Constantine. Here the founder of the city had erected a column of porphyry, the reddish purple stone from Egypt which was reserved for imperial use. On the top of the shaft, almost one hundred seventeen feet above the ground, stood an antique statue of Apollo, with the head of the emperor substituted for that of the god. In the base were Christian relics, as well as the Palladium, the ancient sacred image of Pallas Athene which was supposed to be a pledge of the safety of Rome. The Forum of Constantine contained one of the public clocks of the city (others were in St. Sophia and in the palace).

From Constantine's forum the *Mesê* led to a series of squares which provided centers for so much of the daily life of the city. After Constantine's square came the Forum of Theodosius, containing a column sixty feet high bearing the statue of the emperor who built it. Near this was the Capitolium, imitated from that of old Rome, which housed the University of Constantinople founded by Theodosius II in A.D. 425, with its professors of Greek and Latin grammar, rhetoric, philosophy, and jurisprudence. A public library had been established soon after the foundation of the city and the Emperor Julian the Philosopher (A.D. 361–363) had endowed the Imperial Basilica or law court which possessed a large library of legal works.

The forums continued—the Amastrianum, followed by the Forum of the Ox, and finally the Forum of Arcadius (A.D. 395–408). Here stood one of the tallest and most impressive monumental columns of the city, over one hundred forty feet in height, bearing a statue of the founder of the forum. In a city of hills and valleys such as Constantinople, these tall columns were a particularly effective motif as they rose against the skyline, perpetual memorials of the care which the emperors had taken of the city. The interior of the column of Arcadius contained a spiral staircase of 233 steps leading to a platform below the statue, and from this the visitor had a magnificent view of the city and the sea.

The tour of Constantinople showed that along with the colonnaded streets and the forums, the city exhibited all the characteristic marks of classical urban life. Great care had been taken over the water supply which was so important in the Mediterranean climate. Water had been piped into the city through aqueducts from the hills beyond the walls, and there were cisterns everywhere, both open and covered, for storage of water. The city was well supplied with the public baths which were essential for personal hygiene and health in the hot climate, and also provided centers for social life and recreation. The baths were open at different times for men and women. These establishments used a considerable quantity of water; and water for drinking, cooking, and washing was available to the public free of charge at the fountains in the public squares and at the corners of the streets.

In addition to providing for a good water supply, the government took measures to protect public health. There were public physicians, paid by the government, who treated people who were unable to pay fees, and there were free hospitals maintained by both the government and the Church. A certain amount of care was taken for sanitation, and there were underground masonry drains, fed from the houses through terra cotta pipes, which carried waste water and sewage down to the sea. Burial of dead bodies inside the city was forbidden, except that relics of saints could be preserved in churches, and members of the imperial family might be buried in the Mausoleum attached to the Church of the Holy Apostles. But in spite of all these provisions, disease was common. Dysentery was widespread and was frequently fatal. The city suffered terribly from the bubonic plague which swept over the whole of the empire in A.D. 542 and 543. There were times during the plague when there were 5,000 deaths a day in the capital, and when the visitation was at its worst it was estimated that 10,000 people died every day.

There were in general no fashionable quarters in Constantinople, and the visitor would see wealthy establishments flanked by modest or even poor houses. The houses of the rich were built in the Roman style, of two stories, with a blank wall facing the street, and the rooms opening on a central courtyard containing a fountain and possibly a garden with ornamental trees. Such houses would be built of brick—the long narrow Roman brick which was laid in a plentiful amount of mortar—and faced with cut stone or marble. More modest dwellings might be on the same plan, on a smaller scale, or they might be a series of rooms grouped about a passage entered from the street door. On the side streets, opening off the main thoroughfares, the houses had bow windows projecting over the street, from which the ladies of the family could watch events in the street and keep abreast of their neighbors' affairs. The size of such bow windows or "sunrooms," like the width of the streets, was regulated by law. Occasionally there would be a café or shop with an open front, and here and there the streets opened out into squares with trees growing in them, and fountains.

In this city of 600,000 people the streets were filled with the most varied collection of humanity one could imagine. Aside from foreign visitors, the residents of Constantinople were themselves of mixed origin, just as the empire itself had been cosmopolitan from the beginning. By this time persons of pure Roman or Greek descent were no longer numerous, and most people showed a mixture of blood from all the ancient lands which the empire of Justinian's day embraced, each with its own language and its own culture and traditions. Anatolians descended from the old races of their land, such as the Cappadocians and Phrygians, and further back, the Hittites; Greeks from the home land; Illyrians from the lands along the coast of the Adriatic Sea; descendants of Goths and Celts who had been settled within the empire for several generations now; Copts from Egypt; Syrians; Armenians—all these nations, along with the descendants of the ancient Greeks and Romans, had come together to form a population which called itself "Roman" and spoke Greek. The criterion of citizenship was membership in the Orthodox Church and use of the

Greek tongue. Greek was the common speech throughout the empire, and as the international language of trade, it would enable a traveler to penetrate well beyond the borders of Justinian's territory. In the eastern part of the empire, Latin was now used only in the army, in law, and in the records of some of the government bureaus; and Greek was in fact supplanting Latin as the language of the law.

New blood was constantly coming in from outside the empire. Mercenary soldiers made up a large part of the army—Franks, with other Germans in considerable numbers; Sarmatians, Huns, Gepids, all were attracted by the service, and then, when they retired, sometimes settled within the empire.

It was characteristic of the city that some of its leading figures had not been born there, and did not in fact speak Greek as a mother tongue. Justinian himself, like his uncle Justin, had been born in Illyricum, where Latin was spoken along with the indigenous tongue. Belisarius, Justinian's greatest general, came from the country region of Thrace and Illyricum. Narses, a cabinet official and general, was Armenian. Examples could be found everywhere of newcomers who had made their way to high positions. There was no racial prejudice, and no objection to marriage with persons of foreign origin so long as they possessed the two basic qualifications—orthodoxy and the Greek language. The prejudice was against barbarians who had neither of these essentials of civilization.

The foreign figures who were to be seen throughout the city were sometimes very exotic. Foreign slaves were common, and were to be met everywhere in the streets. But they would attract less attention than the visitors who came to the city from all parts of the world. At once seaport, prosperous commercial city, and center of the world's largest empire, Constantinople drew men from beyond the seas on many errands. Sailors, merchants, and travelers came from all the countries of the Mediterranean and from Britain and the Atlantic coasts of Gaul and Spain. Merchants and diplomatic missions might come from Persia and Arabia, as well as from the lands around the Euxine Sea and from northern Europe and Scandinavia. There were Saracens who lived in the deserts between Syria and Persia, and served as federate allies of the Romans against the Persians. After Justinian's reconquest of North Africa and Italy, visitors from those lands, of Berber, Vandal, and Gothic stock, as well as Italians of Roman blood, might be seen in Constantinople. Strange faces and strange costumes were to be met in all the streets, and exotic tongues heard, and the foreign dress—furs, strange headgear, barbarian trousers, colorful robes—stood out against the plainer tunics and cloaks of the citizens of the empire, and the dark robes of the monks.

The main streets and the squares were filled not only with business but with social life. The people of the eastern cities of the Græco-Roman world had inherited the ancient Greek love of life in the open air. In Constantinople, there were many places in which the citizens could gather in the out-of-doors Mediterranean social life. The streets and the great open forums alone gave ample room for the daily promenade. Friends could also meet in the open colonnaded courtyards before the entrances to the churches, or they could go to walk along the country roads outside the city walls. The water all about the city offered constant enjoyment. One could stroll in the gardens built along the shores or go on the water in rowboats or sailboats. Making one's way up the Golden Horn, crossing to the Asiatic shore of the Bosporus, or sailing north from the city, one could find pleasant gardens, fields, and woods.

In one place or another, the daily outing was indispensable for social and intellectual life, and the long and leisurely conversations of classical Athens continued to delight the citizens of Constantinople. Friends and neighbors on every level of society depended upon one another for the pleasures of walking and talking. The great ones of Constantinople met each other daily in the Augustæum, in front of the Great Palace, to stroll and chat, and examine the offerings of the booksellers who had their stalls in the square. In the winter, the porticoes provided shelter for the daily excursion. In summer everything moved outdoors, and on the flat roofs of the houses one could sleep in the cool night air, and walk in the early morning and the evening to enjoy the view. Poets wrote of the beauties of the city as seen from its roofs.

The public baths were regular meeting places. Restaurants and cafés offered meals or light refreshments, as needed, and one could sit for hours with friends over games which were akin to dominoes and checkers. In summer the tables were set out in the street. Entertainment of almost any kind could be found. In the streets there might be trained animals, jugglers, acrobats, and musicians. The theatres no longer regularly offered classical plays; the ancient dramas had become literary pieces to be studied in schools. Instead, the theatres of Constantinople presented pantomimes, ballets, or burlesque dances, often based on classical myths. The one great center of entertainment for the whole city was the Hippodrome with its chariot races. On major occasions the races lasted all day, with variety shows in the intervals, presenting acrobats, dancers, and exhibitions of wild animals and trained animals. Again, the whole city

would turn out to watch the spectacular parades and processions on the great religious festivals and national holidays, when the sovereigns and the court would pass through
the streets with the patriarch and his suite.

One source of entertainment which Constantinople alone
enjoyed was the week of spectacles provided each year by
the new consul, during the first week of January. The consulship had been the glory of the Roman Republic, and
the most powerful executive office in it. It still retained a
good deal of importance under the early emperors, but it
had gradually been stripped of its real powers and preroga-
tives. Thus in Constantinople, by Justinian's time it had
become a purely honorary office, with one consul in the
eastern half of the empire, the other in the West. In Constantinople, the consul was expected to mark his entry into
office by distributing gifts of money to the people and
offering a week of magnificent public entertainments—
chariot races, exhibitions of wild animals, and theatrical
shows, all offered on successive days following the inaug-
ural procession and ceremony of investiture on January 1.
To his friends in high places, the consul sent costly "con-
sular diptychs," two hinged leaves of ivory carved with
appropriate scenes, serving as mementos of his holding
the office.

As successive consuls in the past had tried to outdo each
other, the cost of holding the office had grown so great
that only a few of the richest men in the empire could
hold it. Before Justinian's reign, the consulship had come
to cost its holder at least 2,000 pounds of gold, and some
spent more. Justinian was consul in 521, during his uncle's
reign, and it is recorded that he spent 4,000 pounds of
gold; in his animal show he exhibited twenty lions and
thirty leopards. Eventually the office became such a bur-

den that no one could undertake it; but the government did not dare to abolish the games, and part of the expense had to be borne by the treasury. After 541 individuals ceased to hold the office and the emperor became perpetual consul.

The visitor would soon realize that, as in every capital, life in Constantinople centered about the government, that is, the imperial court and the bureaucracy. And it was the presence of the government which gave the city an opulence of a kind not to be found in other cities. The economic system of the Græco-Roman world had tended to produce and perpetuate extremes of wealth and poverty, and these were to be seen in any city; but in Constantinople the life of wealth and luxury was even more conspicuous than usual.

At the head of society, of course, was the imperial court. In addition to the revenue from taxes, the enormous estates which were the private property of the crown brought in a considerable income. In the nature of the imperial office it was considered not only appropriate but necessary for the Emperor Justinian and his Empress and their family to live in the most magnificent style, on a scale which corresponded to the exalted position of the Emperor. The court, composed of the Emperor's council, the heads of the army and of the civil service bureaus of the government, the senators, the ecclesiastical dignitaries and other prominent personages with whom the Emperor liked to surround himself, lived in comparable style, though personal display was carefully maintained at a level lower than that of the imperial family. The members of the imperial household—ladies in waiting, chamberlains, ushers, pages, and so on—completed the glittering spectacle.

The official life of the court revolved around a series of ceremonies which had developed into pageants of the most elaborate kind. Audiences granted by the Emperor, receptions of foreign dignitaries, banquets, celebrations of national and religious holidays, when the Emperor gave gifts to the members of the court, occurred in unending succession. On every great festival of the Church calendar there would be special services, either in one of the churches in the palace, or in one of the great churches in the city, such as St. Sophia or the Holy Apostles, and the Emperor and Empress, with the whole court, in full dress robes, would march or ride in procession through the city, to be met at the church by the patriarch with his attendant clergy.

The robes worn by the sovereigns and the court on these occasions—richly embroidered tunics and cloaks ornamented with gold thread and precious stones—turned life at the court into a spectacle of such magnificence that it practically seemed removed from human existence. But this was no mere display of wealth. At all these ceremonies the lavishness of the costumes and the insignia—the crosses and sceptres carried in procession, the imperial crowns, the military standards—were symbols of the glory of the empire. The display also played an important part in diplomacy by giving barbarian emissaries to Constantinople an overwhelming impression of the empire's wealth and power. The well rehearsed manifestation of imperial splendor was permanently recorded in mosaics placed in the ceiling of the new entrance to the Great Palace built by Justinian. The scenes depicted that Emperor's great reconquests of lost Roman territory, in Africa and Italy. The general, Belisarius, was shown returning to the Emperor, bringing rich spoils. In the center stood the Emperor and Empress, rejoicing in their victory over the King of the Vandals and the King of the Goths, who were being led

27

before them as prisoners of war. All about stood the members of the Senate, sharing the Emperor's joy and doing him honor. The mosaic has perished, but one can gain some idea of what it must have been like from the mosaics in the apse of the Church of St. Vitalis in Ravenna, dedicated in A.D. 547, showing the Emperor and Empress and their attendants in their rich robes.

The membership in the imperial circle represented quite different elements. By the time of Justinian, the oldest families of the Roman aristocracy had for the most part died out, and their places had been taken by new families which sometimes were not far removed from their modest origins. Enterprising young men who came to the capital to make their way in the army or the government sometimes rose to high positions, and often made fortunes, for a successful lawyer or general or civil servant could become wealthy. There was an aristocracy of landowners who had built up large estates, especially in Anatolia and Syria. Land was the safest investment for capital, and the large farmers tended to absorb the holdings of their poorer neighbors. The Emperor's friends were rewarded with estates, while the imperial house itself was one of the largest landowners in the empire.

Other members of the aristocracy of the capital had become wealthy as bankers or shipowners, or as contractors supplying the army and the government. The members of families of wealth possessed both town houses—sometimes really small palaces—in Constantinople, and villas in the country, or along the shores of the Bosporus, where they lived in an elegance that dazzled less sophisticated visitors from the western part of the empire. The great families maintained circles of dependents—literary men, tutors, monks, scholars—which were like little courts. Such families were clannish and worked together for the advancement of their relatives.

Family life in the average household was decorous and sober, and the discreet virtues taught by the Church were taken seriously. Sincere honor was paid to the older generation. The grandmother had great authority and it was she who often arranged the marriages of the grandchildren. Young girls before marriage were kept at home and trained in household duties and in the skills necessary for women, such as spinning, weaving, and embroidery. Girls were also trained in academic subjects, and wherever it was possible, they were given the same kind of education that a boy would receive. A girl whose parents could afford tutors could follow all the studies that a boy would pursue at school; but a girl might not attend a school outside the house, and higher education away from home was not open to her. However, as soon as a girl was married, she moved freely everywhere and was the equal of men intellectually and socially; and her family status and property rights were carefully protected by legislation.

As it had always been in the eastern part of the Græco-Roman world, the basic curriculum was the study of the Greek classics. Homer was still the fundamental text. Grammar, rhetoric, and literary exercises all were based on classical models, and boys, after preparation under a tutor or at a private school, would go on to higher studies of philosophy and rhetoric under an individual teacher, at Constantinople or in other centers of learning such as Alexandria or Gaza. A boy would then, if his plans called for it and his resources made it possible, go on to professional training, such as the study of law at the imperial schools at Beyrouth and Constantinople.

In this liberal education, devoted primarily to literature

and philosophy, science played a subordinate part. The technical subjects such as mathematics, physics, medicine, were studied from the philosophical point of view and were still taught, in Justinian's day, from the writings of the ancient masters. Mathematics was studied (as it had been in Plato's day) because it purified the mind and prepared it for the much higher subject of philosophy. Zoology, for example, was a learned study, but it was concerned largely with curious information—the collection of anecdotes about strange and even fantastic animals—and not with true scientific knowledge. In medicine, observed phenomena had to be fitted with the teachings of the ancient authorities.

In all scientific studies a distinction was drawn between the "philosophical" and the "practical" aspects of the subject, and a gentleman might study the former without troubling himself about the latter. Indeed, manual execution was not fitting for a gentleman and was left to artisans; but the artisans were not thought to be capable of studying the theoretical side of their calling. Anything connected with technology was of a much lower status than philosophical and literary pursuits, and science was still a division of philosophy.

Against such a background, technological knowledge, such as would be necessary for the manufacture of machinery, had not advanced. In Constantinople in the reign of Justinian, the principle of the steam engine, for example, was known and applied experimentally, but it occurred to no one to use steam as a working force. Practical application in any case would not have been possible because knowledge of metal working was limited and it was not feasible to construct complicated or delicate machinery. Also, with the traditional use of slave labor and cheap free labor, there was little or no interest in labor-saving machinery.

If a young man wished to become a physician or an engineer or builder, he had to find a practitioner who would take him as an apprentice. The public physicians who cared for the poor and worked in publicly endowed hospitals, were required to train students. Architects and engineers who held government appointments were also required to take apprentices. If, in such circumstances, instruction varied in quality, it did preserve the intimate relationship of teacher and student which ancient education regarded as a basic necessity.

A basic distinction of Byzantine education was that education, as such, never became the exclusive prerogative of the clergy as it did in the western Middle Ages. The old classical tradition of secular education was regarded by the Byzantine people as one of the most precious institutions in their inheritance.

While they lived in the midst of this highly developed intellectual life, with its deep regard for philosophy, the people of Constantinople, from the Emperor and Empress down, were genuinely superstitious. A distinction was made between astrology and the forms of superstition which were taken for granted. Astrologers were looked upon as criminals engaged in fraud, and when found and convicted they were severely flogged and then mounted on camels and paraded through the streets. But superstition was accepted. In part this was due to the lack of progress in scientific knowledge. Natural phenomena were still not fully understood and men who were highly educated for their day lived in terror of the unseen and the unknown. This was the same superstition that had existed throughout the ancient pagan world, and it had never wholly died out, even under the influence of Christianity. To it was now added the Christian belief in the miraculous, especially in healing miracles. There were miraculous images and relics of saints, the touch of which would heal, and there were churches where healings took place. At the far end of the Golden Horn stood an ancient church dedicated to Saints Cosmas and Damian, the saints who had been physicians. Justinian once when seriously ill had been healed when he had gone to this church and the saints had appeared to him in a vision; and in gratitude he had enlarged and beautified the church and it was regularly visited by the sick, who were taken up the Golden Horn in boats. If a sick person slept in such a church, it was possible that he might have a vision and be healed.

Justinian also believed that he had been healed on another occasion by miraculous oil which suddenly flowed from certain holy relics. The robe the Emperor had been wearing, which had been saturated by the oil, was preserved in the palace, both as a testimonial to the incident and because the garment itself might be expected to have healing powers. Presumably the physicians who had been unable to cure the Emperor welcomed this divine intervention.

Any good Christian could, and in fact should, believe in miracles of this kind. There were also, of course, grosser stories of marvels performed by saints and holy men, and some of these it would have been difficult for the sophisticated to accept; but the tales were enshrined in popular lives of the saints and they served a worthy purpose for the edification of simple people.

This general willingness to accept the supernatural grew out of the teaching of the New Testament itself; but it was also possible for a good Christian to believe in demons and sorcery. This relic of paganism was not a characteristic of Constantinople alone. We know, for example, that a patriarch of Antioch was accused of sorcery and had to go to Constantinople to stand trial. He was aquitted, and his accusers were severely punished; but the accusation and the trial were taken seriously.

Procopius, one of the most highly educated men of his time and an experienced man of affairs, accustomed to important responsibilities in the army, believed in omens and dreams and recorded them in his history of Justinian's wars; and in his *Secret History* he has elaborate accounts of demons and witchcraft. Justinian's enemies, we learn from Procopius, put into circulation astonishing stories. Men who had occasion to talk with the Emperor late at night—he was a late worker—declared that he would rise suddenly from the throne and pace up and down, and that suddenly his head would disappear while his body continued pacing. Later the head would return to the body. Or the Emperor's eyes would disappear and his face would become featureless flesh. A monk, coming into the imperial presence to present a petition, saw the Lord of Demons sitting on the throne. Calamities that occurred during Justinian's reign were attributed to demonic action which became possible when the Deity, angered by the Emperor's behavior, withdrew his favor. The Empress Theodora, Procopius says, was a lifelong student of sorcery. She was once bewitched by a member of the court who was dabbling in such matters, and she herself made the Emperor tractable by casting spells on him. Procopius tells all this in a perfectly matter of fact way, and we may be sure that he and many of his friends believed these stories.

Alongside the separate world of the court and the bureaucracy, and the daily life of the well-to-do, there was all the mundane business of the ordinary people of Constantinople.

In its commercial life, Constantinople differed from other cities of the empire chiefly in its greater prosperity as the capital. The city had originally been founded, as Byzantium, for purely business purposes, and when it was transformed into the eastern capital of the empire, it grew to be one of the leading commercial centers of the world, as well as one of the leading manufacturers of luxury goods. The requirements of the members of the government alone would have supported a lively business in the ordinary needs of life. When, in addition, the imperial court and the great houses had to be kept supplied with luxuries of every description, and when merchants and travelers sought costly gifts to take home with them, the city became a center of fine craftsmanship of all kinds.

Raw materials were brought to Constantinople from all over the world and unloaded from the overland caravans, or at the docks and warehouses which lined the Golden Horn. The wonderful opportunities the city offered also attracted artists and craftsmen from all over the empire. Jewelry of the finest design and workmanship, made up of precious stones, niello and incredibly delicate gold work; carved ivory; ivory caskets for jewels and cosmetics; elaborate gold and niello lockets, hollow crosses and boxes for sacred relics; fine cloth; leather goods; books with delicate miniatures and illuminations; copper and bronze work of all kinds—any article of finest workmanship could be produced in Constantinople, for sale to the citizens or export throughout the empire and beyond its borders. Objects which had been brought from Constantinople were admired and imitated throughout the world.

The churches alone of Constantinople and the rest of

the empire required a steady production of gold and silver vessels for use in the liturgy, crosses of jeweled gold or silver, silver or bronze lamps, and reliquaries of richest manufacture for the reception of sacred relics. The book-sellers maintained staffs of calligraphers and artists who produced beautifully copied and richly ornamented Bibles and service books.

The visitor would find the merchants and craftsmen of each type of goods settled together in their little shops, each trade occupying its own street, in the ancient fashion of the oriental bazaar. The craftsmen worked alone, with apprentices or children, and an object was often bought from the man who had made it. Whenever the season per-mitted, work was done, and goods were sold, out of doors, and the bazaars and forums were alive with business.

For the most part, the bazaar quarter lay along the route of the Middle Street between the Augustæum and the Forum of Theodosius. The visitor could inspect rows of shops which sold meat, other streets where fish was sold; and all the other kinds of food—cheese, honey, vegetables, fruit, and so on—were offered, each in its own row of open stalls or shops. Nails would be sold in one part of the city, charcoal in another, shoes in another. The bronze work-ers had their quarter just west of the Augustæum. The bakers' establishments lay along the Middle Street between the Forum of Constantine and the Forum of Theodosius. Horses were sold in the Amastrianum; sheep in the Forum of Theodosius. Perfume sellers had their stalls in the Au-gustæum.

The businesses and crafts were organized in guilds which were rigorously controlled according to the contemporary notion that economic prosperity could be ensured by leg-islation. The son of a guild member was required to follow his father's calling, and attempts to escape such obligations were severely punished.

Everywhere, as one walked about the city, one would see taverns and cook shops, and the air was filled with the scent of charcoal fires. At the great festivals and public holidays, especially Easter, the government provided free meals in the forums. Lambs were roasted whole and the meat was served to anyone who asked for it.

But in the midst of this prosperity the visitor would see everywhere contrasts to the luxury and refinement of the court and the elegant circles which surrounded it. Slavery was an accepted feature of society, and there was a perpetual class of the unemployed, poor free men who often were less well off than some slaves. Slavery, unemployment, and poverty were inherent features of the economic system of the world of those times, and they were looked upon simply as parts of the natural order of things; but they constituted a sad fringe to the solid and well established civilization of the empire.

Slavery, which had existed long before the coming of Christianity, was countenanced by the Church, which itself owned slaves. Christian teaching did something to make their lot easier; masters and slaves were exhorted to remember their obligations to each other, and mistreated slaves could seek asylum in churches. There were laws which protected slaves, up to a certain point, but in general they were at the mercy of their owners. Slaves could be set free by generous masters, or could work for themselves in their spare time and save money to purchase their freedom. Foreign slaves—prisoners of war or captives taken in raids by slave traders—were numerous, as laborers, domestic servants, sometimes artisans.

The records of the construction and endowment of

hospitals, poorhouses, and old people's homes, both at Constantinople and throughout the empire, are testimony to the constant need to provide for the poor and for the sick who could not be cared for by their families. Both the Church and the government made resolute efforts to care for these people, and they were given free meals in the kitchens attached to the large churches. The charitable work of the Church was extensive. Still, in the current conception of the working of the economy, it was not considered possible to do anything to cure unemployment itself. Constantinople was like every other large city in this respect. As the capital, it was the goal of both the ambitious and the unsuccessful. While there was chronic unemployment within the city, people tried continually to come to it, both from the country and from other cities, to find work or to improve their prospects. The authorities tried to keep people from entering the city unless they could prove they had business to be done, but it was not easy to prevent them from getting in illegally. The government built hostels for visitors, both in order to save them from unscrupulous innkeepers, and in order to keep an eye on their activities.

The able-bodied unemployed could be made to work on public construction projects, but at the same time the government thought it necessary to continue the corrupting practice of old Rome and distributed free bread. One of the major problems and responsibilities of the authorities was to maintain a steady supply of grain for the bakeries. As in any Mediterranean land, bread was a principal item in the diet. The grain came from Egypt, and if the fleet of ships bringing it from Alexandria were delayed by bad weather, and if bread were not forthcoming, there would be riots. The bakers' guild was rigorously supervised.

CONSTANTINOPLE

Again on the model of old Rome, the authorities furnished circuses as well as bread; and the Hippodrome was one of the centers of life in Constantinople. Built in the third century by the Emperor Septimius Severus, it was a smaller copy of the Circus Maximus in Rome. Rising beside the palace, the Hippodrome was too long for the hill on which it was placed, and its southern end had to be supported on massive foundations which rose high in the air. Sixty thousand people could be crowded into its thirty tiers of seats. The *spina* or barrier which separated the two sides of the race course was decorated with ancient statues. Two of the monuments were world famous. One, still standing, was the obelisk brought from Egypt by the Emperor Theodosius the Great, a monolith of porphyry eighty-four feet high, mounted on a sculptured base showing the Emperor presiding at the games. The other was the bronze column from Delphi formed of three intertwined serpents, still partially preserved, whose heads had originally supported the gold tripod dedicated to Apollo after the Greek victory at Platæa in 479 B.C. On the side of the Hippodrome toward the palace was the imperial box in which the Emperor and the more distinguished members of the court viewed the races.

The citizens of Constantinople had all the passion of the people of old Rome for chariot races, and the Hippodrome in the capital came to play an even more important role than the circus had in Rome. In Rome, where four chariots usually competed in a race, four parties or factions had grown up—the Greens, Blues, Whites, and Reds—each backing a favorite charioteer. In Constantinople and the other large cities of the East, factions were organized in imitation of those of Rome, and these became so powerful that the government organized them along political lines. Named the *demes* (from *dêmos*, the people), the factions were placed under demarchs, leaders who were responsible to the city administration. The demes were organized like a local militia and could be called on to defend the walls of the city. With their great popular support, they formed a democratic element in an empire which was in principle an autocracy. When a new emperor was to be proclaimed in Constantinople, the demes were summoned to the Hippodrome, where they went through the form of acclaiming the new ruler, thus giving his investiture the appearance of the approval of the people. In time the popularity of the Reds and the Whites declined and the Blues and the Greens remained, more powerful now because there were two parties instead of four. The factions had their own blocks of seats in the Hippodrome, on either side of the emperor's box, and the emperor himself was usually a partisan of one faction or the other.

Out of the athletic rivalry, political rivalry had developed and the factions at various times backed different causes. Ample possibilities were available in such things as the antipathy of aristocrats and plebeians and the hostility of the supporters of orthodox and heterodox religious ideas. Not uncommonly these rivalries reached such intensity that fighting broke out between the factions, sometimes in the Hippodrome during the races, sometimes in the streets when armed bands of the two parties met each other. The government had a monopoly of the manufacture of weapons and they were supposed to be issued only to the troops, but somehow the young men of the factions got hold of them. Since they were in such close, often daily contact with the emperor in the Hippodrome, the demes began to let their grievances and complaints be known through a spokesman, who was permitted to hold a dialogue with an imperial herald who spoke for the emperor, standing in front of the imperial box. Complaints could cover all subjects, from disapproval of an oppressive official to dissatisfaction with the government's policies as a whole. The emperor, though he was in theory an absolute ruler, usually found it wise to listen to what the demes had to say, for there was always the possibility that dissatisfaction might grow into revolution; and so the safety valve was allowed to exist.

Difficult to control, and impossible to suppress, the factions kept the authorities in a constant state of uneasiness. Of course the members of the parties knew this, and swaggered accordingly. They dressed far more elegantly than their social status entitled them to do, and they adopted the fashion of the barbarian Huns in their cloaks and shoes, and in their tunics made with wide billowing sleeves, fastened tightly at the wrist. They also adopted a bizarre headdress. Whereas it was the custom of the day for men to shave, and wear their hair moderately short, the members of the factions wore moustaches and beards, and shaved their hair on the front of the head, letting the remainder grow long and hang down the back, in the Persian style.

It is not surprising that there were armed bands of factionists who went about the streets at night robbing any citizens they met. Prudent men stayed at home after dark, or if they had to go out, left their gold belt buckles and pins at home and wore bronze instead.

Among all the many facilities for social life and amusement in the city, the Hippodrome played a special role. The whole city gathered here for the spectacles officially provided for its entertainment, and for the great public celebrations. People also made their way to the Hippodrome in times of calamity. The triumphal procession of General Belisarius, exhibiting the Vandal captives and the spoils of the reconquest of Roman Africa, ended in the Hippodrome after making its way through the streets of the city, or when an earthquake struck Constantinople, people sought safety in the open arena of the Hippodrome and the patriarch recited a litany for deliverance.

Or the Hippodrome could be the scene of rebellion and slaughter. The episodes in the Hippodrome of the Nika Revolt, in January, A.D. 532, were something no one who lived in Constantinople at the time would soon forget. Some of Justinian's policies created resistance because they seemed hazardous and over-ambitious. In particular, the heavy taxation necessary to support the imperial program provoked a strong reaction everywhere, and Justinian persisted in encouraging the exactions of his unpopular finance minister, John the Cappadocian. All this discontent came to a head in the famous Nika Rebellion—named from the Greek battle cry of the people, *nika, nika,* "conquer! conquer!"—which eventually involved all sections of society. The immediate occasion was a riot of the Hippodrome factions. Severe punishment of the rioters served to bring out all the resentment and discontent of the people, and what had been a riot became in a few days a popular rising. The senators had their own reasons for discontent—they distrusted Justinian and feared his policies—and they joined forces with the people. A plan was made to depose Justinian and put on the throne Hypatius, one of the nephews of the Emperor Anastasius, who had had a claim to the throne when Justin became emperor. When this plot became known, Justinian took the extraordinary step of appearing briefly in the Hippodrome, carrying a copy of the Gospels in his hands, and he swore that he would grant an amnesty and accede to the people's demands. But the crowd in the Hippodrome remained hostile, and it was too late. Some of the mob crowned Hypatius emperor in the Forum of Constantine, and he was later taken to the Hippodrome and seated, as Emperor, in the imperial box. The whole of the building was filled with the insurgents clamoring against Justinian.

The situation seemed nearly out of control, and Justinian was on the point of fleeing the city; but the régime was saved by the resolute action of the Empress and of some of the generals, including the Emperor's faithful friend Belisarius. The generals were able to get detachments of the imperial guards into the Hippodrome in such a way that they would take the rioters by surprise from two sides. Some of the insurgents had arms, but the crowd was so dense that they were of little use. The soldiers proceeded systematically to cut down all the rioters. Contemporary accounts indicate that the official report was that thirty thousand people were killed. The insurrection was wiped out in this dreadful day in the Hippodrome.

Justinian punished the senators less severely than he might have, and the whole episode served to establish his power more firmly. To the people of Constantinople this story was a sad reminder for many years. The citizens of the great capital, many of them prosperous and fortunate, had felt their power and had tried to use it. One part of the living city had attempted to assert its supremacy. But it was really the emperor—one might here say the imperial office—that was supreme. The city and its people must not forget this.

II

THE EMPEROR: *The Emperor's Agents*

IN THE ROMAN FORUM, near the ancient Temple of Saturn, there had stood a column of gilded bronze, the "Gilded Milestone," from which the roads of the empire were measured. This had been the symbolic center of the empire. As the new capital, Constantinople too had a *milion*, or milestone, in the Augustæum, from which the mileage of the roads running from Constantinople was reckoned.

It was fitting that the *milion*, symbolizing the new center of the empire, should stand in the Augustæum, the heart of the capital. But even the *milion* was a modest and impersonal token in comparison with the bronze equestrian statue of the Emperor Justinian which stood upon a column in the center of the square. The statue on its tall shaft of cut stone, showing the Emperor in Homeric armor and carrying the symbol of his rule, the globe surmounted by the cross, was a commanding image. Dominating the square on which stood St. Sophia, the palace and the Senate House, and the Hippodrome, the statue typified the paramount place of the emperor in the midst of these national tokens of Church, State, and People.

An imperial statue on a stone shaft was a familiar feature of any Roman city. Several of Justinian's predecessors—Constantine the Great, Theodosius the Great, Arcadius, Marcianus—stood on their handsome columns in the different quarters of the city. Everyone in Constantinople saw them every day, and together they served as perpetual witnesses of the strength of the empire and the power—and responsibility—of the imperial office.

In this city, of course, the oldest imperial statue was that of Constantine the Great, but Constantine himself was the heir of old political traditions, some of which, indeed, had roots older than the time of Augustus, the founder of the Principate and the first Roman Emperor (27 B.C.—A.D. 14). The concept of one-man rule, introduced in the time of Augustus, grew gradually but continuously under his successors the Julio-Claudians, through the time of the Severan emperors and down to the rulers of the fourth and fifth centuries. The *princeps* or first citizen represented an idealized ruling figure in which power was combined with responsibility. The emperor by his office was elevated above common mortals, and the eminence of his position in the state and in human society was such that it could only be recognized by a formal worship which was paid to him as—officially—a quasi-divine being. This worship was essentially a declaration of political allegiance which served to bind together the diverse ethnic groups within the empire, with their widely differing indigenous religions and national histories.

This form of imperial rule was accompanied by token survivals of democracy. In principle, the imperial office was open to anyone whose merits made him fit for it. The Senate continued to exist, at least in name. A new emperor had to be acclaimed by an assembly of the people, even if their assent was a mere formality. More important, the new ruler was also acclaimed on his accession by the army; and this was a political reality, for no ruler could have kept himself on the throne without the support of the troops.

After the trying and dangerous years of the third century, when the empire was struggling with its foreign and domestic dangers, the imperial office gained new prestige from the labors of Aurelian and Diocletian. It was in part by adding new attributes to the emperor's official personality that the state was strengthened. Aurelian perceived that the empire as a whole would gain political stability if the divine element in the official conception of the emperor were heightened and developed into a new form which could meet with universal acceptance among his subjects. Here he was utilizing an old concept of rulership. The figure of the hero or heroic man had long been a familiar one, and from this to the idea of divinization of a human being—a man who could be expected to show divine attributes—was a natural step. The ruler as a god was a well-understood concept, and with the growing role of the eastern section of the empire, oriental mysticism became more familiar and more accepted. Here the cult of the Sun-God, already a powerful force in Syria, offered an ideal opportunity, and the ruler now became identified, in the official political theory, with Apollo. Aurelian also bore for the first time a title which implied his true divinity, *deus et dominus natus*, "Born Lord and God."

The new theory of the nature of the emperor and of his power answered a need, and it was further elaborated by Diocletian. According to current religious ideas, every Roman had a divine "companion" or guardian deity who watched over him. An emperor, as befitted his station, had as his "companion" one of the more powerful gods. The emperor was thought of as being in direct communication with the god who was his guardian. Various rulers might adopt different divinities, such as Jupiter, Apollo, Hercules. In each case the direct protection of the divine patron enabled the ruler to offer his subjects a reassuring doctrine of the source of his power.

At the same time, in order to give further prestige to the sovereign, practices were borrowed from the ceremonial of the oriental courts, where the ruler traditionally had been an aloof and mysterious figure. The emperor began to be an invisible monarch seldom seen outside his palace, and inaccessible to ordinary mortals. His subjects had to prostrate themselves in his presence, and when he appeared in public it was as an impassive and awesome figure. The crowds in the streets were ordered to cheer as he passed.

It was such a concept of the imperial office that Constantine the Great inherited. He continued the policy of Diocletian in centralizing the government, strengthening the bureaucracy and the army, and setting up a close state control over the whole economy. Production and commerce were carefully regulated. All this was an attempt to conserve the resources of the state and use them primarily for defense and for the support of the government. According to the economic and political ideas of those days, the best way to save the empire was to turn it into a corporative state under an absolute ruler.

Constantine was engaged in this task when he was converted to Christianity. His conversion at once raised serious political questions. As Roman emperor he had been *pontifex maximus*, chief priest of the pagan state religion. He was officially identified with Apollo. How could an emperor who was a Christian fill these posts? What were his Christian subjects to think of their emperor who held his office in a long succession of pagan rulers endowed with charismatic authority? A Christian ruler, ruling Christians, must be very different from this. If there was to be a Christian Roman Empire, it must have its own Christian theory of the nature of the ruler and the source of his power.

The theory was set down in writing by Bishop Eusebius of Cæsarea, one of Constantine's closest ecclesiastical advisers. Eusebius was a scholar and he knew the sources thoroughly. The theory that he worked out, while shaped for a new purpose, took into account the best elements of several traditions. It was obviously necessary to keep, if possible, certain features of the existing ideology of the Roman Emperor, for one could not expect the whole empire to be converted to Christianity at once. But there were elements in the old Hellenistic theory of kingship which had affinities to Christian ideas. The Hellenistic ruler had been described as father, shepherd, benefactor, preserver, and savior of his people. He was God Manifest. He was Law Incarnate and as such was the source of justice and clemency. This concept of an ideal ruler fitted well with Christian ideas. Eusebius' doctrine defined the Christian emperor as the heir of both the Roman and the Hellenistic traditions, and as the elect of God, ruling on earth as the vicegerent and representative of God. Earth was a counterpart of heaven, and the emperor played on earth the role of God in heaven. He was responsible to God for the welfare of his people in every sphere, political, material, spiritual. It was his responsibility to prepare his people for the Kingdom of God and to lead them to it. He ruled through the guidance and the inspiration of God, and God dictated his actions to the emperor. Just as there is one God, with one divine law, so there is one earthly ruler and one earthly law. The Logos of the Holy Trinity, that is, the Divine Spirit, is the companion of the ruler and is the messenger and interpreter of the divine will. This gives the emperor power and responsibility at the same time, and gives his decisions and actions a divine sanction. Constantine had himself represented on his coins, in profile, his gaze directed upward to receive the message of the Deity.

Thus God is the source of the emperor's power and his wisdom, just as the Hellenistic and Roman deities had been supposed to be the sources of the power and wisdom of the rulers of those times. The Christian emperor, as his predecessors had been, was the chosen one of God. Of course he was still elected by the Senate and acclaimed by the people and the army, but it was God who brought the future ruler into being, guided his career, and instigated his election.

Eusebius also set forth the ruler's function from the divine point of view. Since only God, he writes, is perfectly good and wise and strong, and is the origin of justice, the source of reason and wisdom, the fountain of light and life, the dispenser of truth and virtue, and the author of kingship itself and of all rule and authority, it is plain that the emperor, as the mediator between God and man, possesses all these virtues and qualities automatically, *ex officio*. He forms his soul, Eusebius says, by means of the royal virtues, into a counterpart of the kingdom above. A new epithet was used of the Emperor, *philanthropos*, "lover of mankind." The same epithet was regularly applied to Christ in the services and prayers of the Church.

This theory represented Constantine's own religious conviction and experience, and it was so exactly suited to the ideas of the day and to the needs of the state and society that it remained unaltered for centuries, and made its contribution to the political ideas of both East and West in later times. But if the theory was one which would live far into the future, it was not possible for it to be fully realized at once. The Roman world remained partly pagan for some time. Constantine's successors were immersed in the problems of the moment, secular and theological. Theodosius the Great (A.D. 379–395), a religious and conscientious man, carried the concept of the imperial office further by issuing imperial legislation to enforce orthodoxy in religious belief. But succeeding emperors were again absorbed by their special problems. One of the great questions, brought into the foreground by Theodosius' policy, was the relation of the emperor and the Church. In a matter which involved the interests and the jurisdiction of both, which should be supreme? This question was well understood, and now and again there would be an occasion when an emperor might assert his claim to supreme responsibility and authority, or the Church might try to establish its ascendancy over the state. Yet the concept of the emperor remained undiminished, if not always fully realized.

This was the office to which Justinian found he would succeed. It was not long before a new statement of the emperor's powers was published. This was a collection of seventy-two paragraphs of advice to the emperor, composed by the Deacon Agapetus, a member of the staff of the Church of St. Sophia. The tone of the treatise makes it plain that it was written soon after Justinian became sole emperor. Whether it was produced at Justinian's behest, or composed on the initiative of Agapetus, we cannot determine. In either case it is a classic epitome in which we can see what the new Emperor's subjects officially thought of his function—or what it was desired that they should think of it. Agapetus would have been satisfied with the success of his work in antiquity; and something like twenty editions of it were printed in Europe in the sixteenth century.

The first sentence of the treatise contains the all-important statement that the emperor's office comes from God. He rules under the laws, and is ever watchful for their enforcement. The emperor is an image of piety, and since he was created by God himself, the emperor owes his creator a return for his gift. Nothing is more honorable for a man than to act as a "lover of mankind," and the emperor should act so as to please God who gave him his good will. The emperor must keep his soul in a state of purity, since a pure soul will be able to see what needs to be done. The ruler will be responsible if, through error, he brings any injury to the state. The emperor's mind must be even and firm in the midst of changing circumstances. Piety is the greatest crown of a ruler.

Agapetus returns to the old classical theme that the best government is one in which the philosopher is a ruler, or the ruler a philosopher; he praises Justinian for his study of philosophy and for his love of wisdom and fear of God. The emperor must be temperate and just, and benevolent toward the needy. He will show his power to his enemies, but his love to his subjects. Because no man on earth is superior to him, he must behave as God does, and never become angry. He must never transgress the laws, since there is no one on earth who can force him to obey them.

The author goes on to say that the emperor must seek the will of God through both study and prayer. He must take care not to appoint evil men to office since he will be responsible to God for what they do. For the same reason he must not yield to the flattery of friends. Every man who strives for salvation must make haste to seek the help which comes from above; and this must be true of the emperor before all, since he has to care for all men. If the ruler is lord over all human beings, he is, like all of them, the servant of God.

Agapetus dealt only by implication with the question of the emperor's relation with the administration of the Church on earth. Justinian's view—in theory—of this relationship is stated in the preamble of an imperial decree on the ordination of bishops, priests, and deacons issued in A.D. 535. This was probably composed by Justinian himself.

The things of greatest importance among men [the decree begins] are the gifts of God, given from on high by his love of mankind, namely priesthood and imperial authority. The first renders service in divine matters, the other governs and takes thought for the earthly aspects of human life. Both proceed from one and the same source, and both make human life fairer. Nothing, then, will be a matter of greater concern to rulers than the honorable position of the clergy, especially since the clergy continually pray to God on behalf of the rulers. If the priesthood is blameless in every respect, and is worthy to stand freely before God, and if the imperial office rightly and fittingly adorns the polity which has been entrusted to it, there will be a well omened concord which will bestow every good thing upon the human race. We therefore have the highest concern both for the true doctrines of God and for the honorable position of the clergy, and we believe that if they keep that honorable estate, there will come to us, through it, the greatest good things as a gift from God, and we believe that we shall hold firmly the things we now have, and obtain the things which have not yet come to us. All things will be done fairly and fittingly, if the beginning of the undertaking is worthy of God and pleasing to him. We believe that this will be the case, if observance is maintained of the holy canons which were handed down by the apostles, those witnesses and servants of the word of God, who are justly praised and revered, and which have been guarded and interpreted by the holy fathers.

Thus, while tradition created a body of duties for the emperor, it fashioned an official personality as well. The man who was, in Agapetus' words, called to be "Lord over all and servant of God," had to possess a whole catalogue of public virtues—justice, moderation, bravery, self control, love of learning, benevolence toward mankind—which would inevitably have their counterparts in his private life. Constantly mirrored and praised in literary compositions, such as Agapetus' address, this official personality was also expressed in an imperial iconography which was a prominent element in all media of art throughout the empire. The emperor's image was constantly before his subjects, on coins and in statues, mosaics, paintings, and textiles. An official portrait of the emperor was placed in every court-room in the realm and in the offices of all the major government functionaries. The presence of the image indicated that the judge or official who sat beneath it was acting as the direct representative of the sovereign. Oaths were taken before the portrait. To affront it or do it physical damage was lèse majesté.

The emperor's subjects would also have constantly before them, in the open air and in public buildings, including churches, pictures and statues of the emperor in which he was shown performing his historic functions. He was depicted as victor over the empire's enemies; receiving the homage both of his subjects and of the defeated barbarians; making offerings to Christ; presiding at the games in the Hippodrome; and so on. The Church had long used pictures of this kind for teaching purposes and as aids in devotion, and the imperial art served the monarchy in a comparable way. Production of this imperial art naturally centered in Constantinople—we may be sure that the emperor's own approval was necessary for the major compositions—and the influence of the style followed in the capital spread through the remainder of the empire, and even beyond its limits.

Such were the official views of the imperial office, and the traditional vehicles of propaganda, when Justinian became emperor. These were the resources and the immense prestige he inherited, and this was the figure he was supposed to be. What did he himself bring to his office and what would he do with his powers?

Justinian had been more fortunate than many emperors in the circumstances through which he was able to prepare for his career. Justin was already 66 years old when he became emperor in A.D. 518 and during the nine years of his uncle's reign Justinian had been recognized as the Emperor's chief adviser. In effect he had been a power behind the throne, directing the affairs of the empire, though Justin did not co-opt his nephew as colleague until his own health began to fail, in the last year of his reign. This meant that Justinian had had nine years of study and preparation, beginning when he was about 36 years old, and that he had become sole emperor at the height of his powers, at about the age of 45.

During these nine years of anticipation Justinian had had the best opportunities to learn the workings of the government and to observe all the problems of state and society, without as yet having the full responsibility himself. Even Justinian's enemies gave him credit for being a prodigious worker, and his brilliant and inquisitive mind took him into everything.

The problems of the empire which Justinian had to study had been growing for a long time. No one could claim that the Roman Empire still enjoyed the prestige of its greatest days, under Augustus, for example, or the Antonine emperors. There had been significant territorial losses. Britain, Gaul, Spain, North Africa, and even Italy itself, with Rome, had been occupied by the barbarians whom the empire's armies had been too weak to keep out. The eastern portion of the empire remained intact, but Persia was always a threat on the Mesopotamian frontier.

This territorial reduction had been matched by internal weaknesses. Man power had been declining as unprosperous times reduced the size of families. The empire was no longer able to furnish all the soldiers needed for its armies, and everywhere in the streets of Constantinople one saw Germans, Slavs, and other barbarians who now made up a large proportion of the army.

In some ways the most serious threat to the whole state and its civilization was the internal dissension between the various ethnic groups in the eastern part of the empire. In Syria and Egypt there had been a powerful resurgence of nationalistic feeling. Some element of national pride was inherent in those lands of non-Greek and non-Roman stock, and this pride had now been called out in all its strength. The people of Syria and Egypt inevitably had religious emotions different from those of the Greeks and Romans, and in the theological disputes over the nature of Christ which had been occupying the Church since the fourth century, the Syrians and the Coptic Christians of

Egypt chose to differ from the orthodox beliefs of Constantinople. Religious disagreement inevitably became associated with racial and linguistic differences, and dissent and heresy were made nationalistic slogans. In Syria and Egypt, every celebration of the Eucharist, with its text modified to reflect local doctrines, became a national demonstration. Justinian, like any intelligent observer in Constantinople (some of the observers had been far from intelligent!) could see that nationalism was growing into separatism.

Any one of these problems of the empire would have been formidable enough by itself. An emperor might have an honorable reign if he simply maintained the existing status and prevented further deterioration. Or he could devote himself to one or two problems, as the Emperor Anastasius had done. Anastasius, a financial expert in the Treasury before he became emperor, had been notably successful during his reign in building up a cash reserve. He had also attempted to settle the theological problem, but here he had had no success.

But Justinian was not content with the notion of keeping the empire going, while making efforts at improvement here and there as occasion arose. Seeing the problems as parts of a whole, he determined to deal with them all together. And his program was not merely a fresh effort to cope with the ills of the state. He soon made it plain that what he intended was a comprehensive plan for renewal—a *renovatio*—of the Roman Empire as a whole. This was to be a return to the empire's great days, a revival of all its ancient strength and its ancient glories. The promptness with which the parts of this program were put into motion after he became sole emperor shows that he had been thinking about these plans for some time.

CONSTANTINOPLE

In Justinian's day, one could analyze the empire and its civilization into three main elements, each representing a tradition which had made its distinctive contribution to the whole. The Roman component represented a tradition of pre-eminence in law, government, and the army. Through these, peace and prosperity once had been brought to the whole civilized world, and the government had stood for stability and strength which were never questioned. Alongside this was the Hellenistic tradition, representing the Greek achievement in education, literature and philosophy, an achievement which had been kept alive and handed on in an unbroken line. The third element, of course, was Christianity, the newest component, which had dominated and reshaped the others and had set the state, society, and civilization off in a new direction.

In each of these elements a student like Justinian could see both the strength and the present problem; and if the problems could be solved, Justinian believed, and if the three elements each could be brought to the condition in which it could make its best contribution, then the result would be a Christian Roman Empire—an empire both Roman and Christian and Hellenic—which would reach a higher state of fulfilment and perfection than the state had ever known. This would be the completion of the work begun by Constantine and Theodosius. The state would be renewed, but its renewal would derive its strength both from its Christian consciousness and from its link with the achievement of Greek and Roman antiquity.

In those days, any student of Greek and Roman history believed in the excellence of the accomplishment of the great men of the past. The masters of philosophy, literature, law, and government represented the highest degree of human endeavor, and their achievements were not to be surpassed. Since the forefathers had already reached the heights of human intellectual power, the best civilization would be one which turned to their accomplishment for its own strength. The whole educational system represented this conviction, and the results of the system seemed good. Education and civilization was not static and repetitious; they found in the great figures of the past what they thought were the best models for the present.

What Justinian's education had been like is not recorded, though we may be sure that Justin saw to it that his nephew had the best possible opportunities. The uncle had come to Constantinople on foot from Illyricum with two other young men, all of them hoping to join the army; and when Justin became prosperous enough to send to Illyricum for his nephew, it must have given him real pleasure to think that the young man could have the schooling which he himself had never had (some people said the old Emperor was illiterate, and while such a thing was possible, it was probably malicious gossip in this case). His career shows how completely Justinian had assimilated the wonderful civilization he had found in Constantinople. Indeed it was not difficult for that civilization to master the people who came to know it, and the intelligent young man from the provinces, under the patronage of his distinguished and influential uncle, would not be slow to see what it was that he might inherit. The city of Constantinople, merely in its physical aspect, would teach a young man like Justinian much.

If Justin and Justinian had not been emperors, others would have come to the throne—the nephews of the Emperor Anastasius, for example. Emperors such as these might have been men who had been born and bred in the civilization of Constantinople. They would have taken its existence for granted, as they would have taken for granted their duty to nourish it and hand it on. But when the ruler was not a native, but came from outside, as Justinian did, the city was there, as the repository and transmitter of the tradition, always ready to play its role and to teach the tradition to those who came to it. Justinian was far from being the only man to whom the city had acted as a teacher in this way; but in him the city had a singularly apt pupil.

By the time Justinian became emperor, he realized fully the great prestige the office carried with it and he also was able to visualize the Christian state which might be brought into being. It was as the center of this Christian state that Constantinople had been founded, but the state, Justinian saw, had not yet been brought to completion. Christianity had necessarily to make its way slowly, but Justinian believed that the time had come when the full potentialities of the Christian Roman Empire could be realized. Justinian thought that he could complete the process begun by Constantine, and he had a clear idea as to how this was to be done. To him, his program was not a new one; it was the fulfilment of a divinely ordained course.

It was not only in the opportunities he had had for the preparation of his career that Justinian was fortunate. He enjoyed good health (and good luck) and lived to be 83. This meant that having become Emperor in his best middle years, he reigned for thirty-eight years. If the period of his uncle's reign is included, Justinian controlled the Roman Empire for forty-seven years.

There seem to have been no striking physical qualities which made Justinian an imposing imperial figure. He was neither tall nor short, but of medium height; and he was inclined to be portly. His face was round, and not displeasing. He was thought to have a marked resemblance to the portraits of the Emperor Domitian. He had a ruddy coloring, and kept his color even after he had fasted for two days, as he frequently did. Whether from natural inclination, or from anxiety about his figure, he ate sparingly, and never drank more than a small amount of wine. Religious fasts he kept strictly, especially at Easter, and he would then live for two days on water and a few herbs. He slept little, especially during the fasts, and spent the nights working, or walking about the palace.

Even people who disliked or feared Justinian recognized that he was easily approachable and invariably kind and polite to everyone with whom he had dealings. He never allowed himself to show anger but always spoke gently, even when anyone else would have been provoked. He talked gladly with anyone, even people of the lowest station.

Justinian might well have made a conventional and advantageous marriage with some daughter of a prominent family. Instead he chose Theodora, a woman of very lowly antecedents but with a quick intelligence and great energy. In the crisis of the Nika Riot, she was more courageous than the Emperor. She had real ability and worked conscientiously at her task as empress, though she sometimes seems to have followed her own interests and she often exercised undue influence over the Emperor. She made enemies and there were many unpleasant stories about her early life. It was said that she was the daughter of a man who had been employed by the Green faction as keeper of the animals which were exhibited at the public spectacles. It was also said that she had been an actress and entertainer. It seems certain that some of the stories told about Theodora could not have been true; but there must have been some basis for such reports. In any case, it seems true that the Empress Euphemia, Justin's wife, would not allow Justinian to marry Theodora, and that the marriage took place only after the old Empress' death.

The portraits of Theodora that have been preserved show an attractive, even beautiful, face. By contrast with her husband's abstemious habits she enjoyed the luxuries an empress could command, and spent a great deal of time bathing and dressing. She enjoyed good food and she slept a great deal, in the day time as well as at night. She took great pleasure in living on the seashore and spent a good bit of time at suburban villas and palaces, where her suite did not always find themselves comfortable.

Theodora died in A.D. 548, when she was 50 or less, of cancer, which, we are told, had spread through her whole body. Justinian was then 66, and he was a widower for seventeen years.

Behind the emperor stood an army of government officials and civil servants. This was literally an army, for the civil service was organized along military lines and was in fact termed *militia*, "military service." Its members wore a uniform of military type, with badges of office and rank. The emblem of the service itself was the belt, of military style, and entering or leaving the service was spoken of as "taking the belt" or "giving up the belt." The higher officials, like the higher army officers, wore belts of gold. The bureaucrat was thus a "soldier" engaged in the personal service of the emperor.

The civil service as it was centered in Constantinople in Justinian's day went back to the reforms of Diocletian and Constantine, but, like so many other features of the Byzantine State, its origins were much earlier. The Roman emperors had found that the administration of the empire, with its widely separated provinces, required a trained and permanent staff of public functionaries. These employees and career officials served under the emperors and under the provincial governors and the chiefs of bureaus and services who sometimes held office only for a brief period. The bureaucratic system inevitably carried within itself the dangers of inefficiency and corruption, but it did provide a continuity and an accumulation of professional experience which gave a measure of stability to the administration.

Diocletian and Constantine, in their plans to reform the government and centralize its power, saw that a reorganized and expanded civil service would be a valuable adjunct in their projected authoritarian state, in which the administration would control every activity of the state and its citizens. Centralization had become necessary not only because of the general decay of the administrative machinery but because of the weakness of the municipal governments which had traditionally been responsible, through the services of the citizens, for local administration, public works and public services. With the decline of the empire's economy as a whole, the local citizens were no longer able to share these responsibilities, and the central government had increasingly to take over both the administration and the financial responsibility for the affairs of the cities. This aid was important in the eyes of the rulers who were seriously concerned for the maintenance of city life as the best expression of civilization.

The reorganization of Diocletian and Constantine did nothing to stop the innate tendency of the bureaucracy to enlarge itself. Constantine's successors did what they could to check overexpansion and corruption, but perfection was not to be had. The system grew cumbersome, and more and more difficult to control; but against this could be counted its merits in providing continuity in the functioning of the vast and complex machine, and in producing a staff of trained permanent functionaries. By the reign of Justinian, this had become the only way in which the government of the empire could be assured. The alternative would have been the revival of the local municipal governments, but by the reign of Justinian this would have been economically impossible.

The basic characteristics of the civil service corresponded to the nature of the emperor's own office. Since the sovereign, in principle, was the sole and supreme ruler, all the members of the state services, soldiers as well as civil employees, were direct agents of the emperor, carrying out his personal wish, which was the law of the state. All appointments were made by the emperor in person, or in his name, and every member of the bureaucracy, from the highest to the lowest, was a representative of the emperor and was personally responsible to him. The emperor could, if he wished, go over the head of a higher official and communicate directly with a subordinate. The directness and immediacy of the link between the emperor and all his officials had the effect of mitigating to some extent the tendencies of the system to become rigid and inefficient.

The position of the emperor was made plain by the way in which the functions of the government were centered in the Great Palace. The palace was not merely the residence of the emperor and his family. Meetings of the emperor's advisory council were held there, and the emperor's personal secretariat also worked in the palace. The close personal relationship was emphasized by the fact that all the high officials whose duties placed them in direct communication with the emperor were given honorific titles and ranks as members of the imperial court, so that by virtue of their official appointments they also held membership and precedence in the emperor's household.

The government was constructed like a pyramid whose apex was the person of the emperor. Since the emperor himself communicated directly with the department heads, there was no provision for a prime minister standing between the sovereign and his officials, though from time to time an individual might become sufficiently influential to be in effect a prime minister.

Justinian, completing a process which had actually been begun by Constantine, tried to secure closer control over the whole machinery by dismembering departments into smaller divisions with a greater number of chiefs who were directly responsible to the emperor. The effect was to give increased importance to the officials in the palace.

The chief of the palatine offices, and of the imperial household, was the master of the offices. He was in charge of the emperor's secretariat and of the court ceremonies and audiences, including the reception of foreign ambassadors. He was also director of the imperial secret police. One of his most important duties was the supervision of the imperial postal system, which maintained communications with all parts of the empire by means of relay stations on all the major roads which provided saddle horses and carriages for couriers and traveling officials. The master of the offices was in effect both a minister of the interior and a minister of foreign affairs, and his duties made him the chief dignitary in the civil hierarchy.

A second official who was in immediate association with the emperor was the chancellor *(quæstor)* of the palace, who was the emperor's chief judicial officer. He drafted and circulated the laws issued by the emperor, and received the petitions which were addressed to the emperor as the supreme court of appeal.

In each major geographical division of the empire, such as the eastern provinces, Africa, Illyricum, and Italy, the provinces were grouped into prefectures, each administered by a prætorian prefect who was in charge of all civil matters within his territory, and was also responsible for the supply and pay of the troops. The prætorian prefect of the East, who was the most important of the prefects, had his residence in Constantinople in direct collaboration with the emperor.

The financial operations of the government were complicated. There was what amounted to a central treasury which received the public taxes, the customs duties, and the income from the state-owned mines. This office also administered the mints. In addition there was an office known as the Private Estates which managed the crown domains which were the official property of the emperor and received the income from them, which was considerable. Finally, each prætorian prefect had his own treasury from which he paid the officials and the troops in his territory.

The military establishment was headed by the masters of the soldiers, who were the generals in command of the troops in the various parts of the empire. They were directly dependent on the emperor, and took precedence immediately after the prætorian prefects and the city prefect of Constantinople. Two of the masters were permanently in residence in Constantinople so that the emperor had the military forces at his immediate disposition. Justinian himself had served as a master of the soldiers during his uncle's reign.

As the capital, Constantinople had a special form of government and did not belong to a province, as other cities did. It was governed by the prefect of the city, who wore the ancient Roman toga as a sign of his office. In the affairs of the capital, he was the supreme authority after the emperor himself. He was responsible for the police, the fire department, the water supply, provision of the food supply, supervision of markets, shops, and guilds, control of public gatherings, inspection of banks. He was in charge of all judicial proceedings within the city. His office was one of the most important in the empire, and any failure of his to keep order might result in an outbreak which could threaten the stability of the government itself.

The highest officials formed the Imperial Council which met regularly and at frequent intervals in the palace. Though he was in theory absolute ruler, the emperor sought the advice of these experts, and the council had a major influence on the affairs of the state.

Each of the principal ministers and military commanders had a personal staff, and each division and office of the government had a numerous personnel, all carefully graded and assigned to duties. When Justinian organized the administration of Roman Africa after it had been recovered from the Vandals, the prætorian prefect of Africa had a staff of 396 in the various bureaus of his office, and each of the seven provincial governors had a staff of 50. Each office had to have a fixed table of organization, for there was keen competition for posts, and the head of an office was inevitably tempted to enlarge his staff as much as possible. In addition to the occupants of authorized positions there were "supernumeraries," applicants for positions who were allowed to do minor jobs while waiting for an opening. Sometimes the regular members of the staffs would hire supernumeraries to do their work for them. We hear of one office in which there were 224 authorized employees and 610 supernumeraries, and there were so many of these aspirants that the number of supernumeraries permitted to a given office had to be regulated by law.

The attraction of the civil service was not so much the salaries (which in the lowest grades were very small) as the fees which the officials in every echelon were able to collect from the public for all legal and financial transactions. The taxpayer even had to pay the tax collector a fee for receiving the tax from him. These fees had originally been bribes or tips, and when it was found impossible to suppress them, they were regulated by law. The fees were indeed so profitable, on top of the salaries, that aspirants were willing to pay substantial sums for civil service appointments, and they would sometimes borrow money on mortgage to pay for a post. A retiring official might sell his office, and some positions were officially for sale by the government. There was no retirement age, and a functionary might be senile by the time he reached the top of his own particular ladder. In such cases elderly officials might pay deputies or supernumeraries to do their work for them. The emperors made every effort to secure retirements and to keep the functionaries moving up the ladder. The members of the various services were all intensely loyal to their own departments, and correspondingly jealous or scornful of other bureaus. We hear of the devotion to forms and reports of the senior specialists, and of their resistance to innovations in office procedure. One of the notable characteristics of the bureaucracy was the respect which was paid to learning and literary scholarship, and in the higher grades literary skill contributed to one's advancement.

Even though a civil service which was so organized was in danger of developing into a class more concerned with its own interests than with those of the empire, the bureaucracy still performed, more or less efficiently, its function of collecting revenues and keeping the machinery of the government working in a large empire in which communications were sometimes slow and difficult. Moreover the fashion in which the machinery functioned directly in the name of the emperor was important for the stability of the whole state. All documents were dated by the years of the emperor's reign, and oaths were sworn in the presence of an official portrait of the emperor. In return the ruler was responsible for the work of his subordinates. The Deacon Agapetus warned Justinian that he would be accountable to God for any wrong done by his officials. Justinian himself was able to find valuable civil servants, and when he found them, he kept them in office for long periods. Indeed the system was essentially an extension of the emperor's official personality, and in this respect at least it might be looked upon as an element of strength in the empire.

III

THE ROMAN TRADITION: *Law*

On August 1, A.D. 527, the Emperor Justin died from the effects of an old wound in the foot, and Justinian became emperor. On February 13, A.D. 528, an imperial decree appointed ten jurists to compile a new codification of the statute law.

This was the prompt beginning of an undertaking which was to be one of Justinian's most lasting monuments. There was an urgent need for a new code. The last codification, issued under Theodosius II in A.D. 438, contained a number of enactments which by Justinian's day had become obsolete or had been modified. Also, of course, a large number of new laws had been made since the Code of Theodosius had appeared.

But there was much more involved than a routine editing of the law. As the empire had developed into an absolute monarchy, the people had ceased to be the source of the law, which had once been made in the representative assemblies, later in the Senate. The emperor had ultimately become the only source of legislation, as well as the final place of appeal. Law was the Emperor's personal pronouncement, his individual fiat. It followed that the emperor, by virtue of his office, was responsible not only for the promulgation of the law, but for the way in which it was interpreted and enforced. Here the sovereign had one of his most conspicuous responsibilities, and it was here that the power to pronounce laws must be matched by the imperial virtues of forbearance, gentleness, and clemency toward his subjects—the virtues which were summed up in the term *philanthropia* or love toward mankind.

Thus in ordering a new codification of the law so soon after his accession Justinian was not only acknowledging his responsibility but making it plain that he would discharge that responsibility on the most equitable basis possible. Here his regime was to mark an immediate advance over the rule of his predecessors, who had known the need for a review of the law but had not attempted it.

Codification of the law had a further significance, one that would mean a great deal in Justinian's plans for his reign. The development of law, public and private, had been from the earliest days of their history one of the most conspicuous achievements of the Roman people, and it had always been acknowledged that their universal system of law was one of their greatest gifts to the civilized world. The heritage of Roman law represented an unbroken tradition which continued down to Justinian's own time, and preservation and renewal of this heritage, the Emperor perceived, offered a fruitful possibility of emphasizing one of the major roots of the empire's strength. Here was a way in which Justinian could remind his people of their share in the political and social achievement of their ancestors. Justinian in his own legal writings, preserved in many places throughout his legislation, spoke of the authority of the old laws which were ancient but still living; he wrote admiringly of "faultless antiquity," *inculpabilis antiquitas*, and of "the venerable authority of antiquity," *veneranda vetustatis auctoritas*.

As an initial step in Justinian's plan for the renewal of the empire as a whole, the purging and codification of the law promised a result which would be widely known and

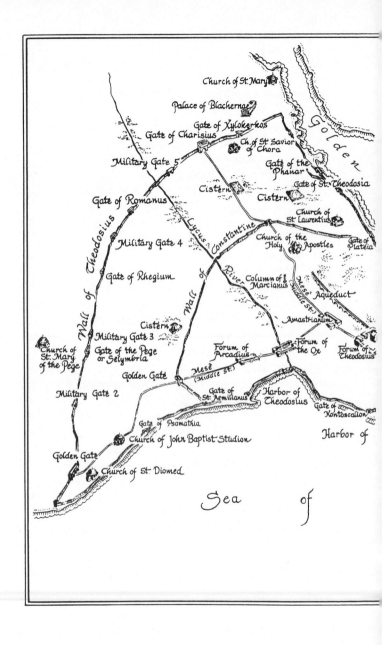

Church of St. Mary

Palace of Blachernae

Gate of Xylokerkos

Gate of Charisius

Ch. of St. Savior of Chora

Military Gate 5

Gate of the Phanar

Gate of St. Theodosia

Cistern

Cistern

Gate of Romanus

Church of St. Laurentius

Wall of Theodosius

Lycus River

Wall of Constantine

Military Gate 4

Church of the Holy Apostles

Gate of Plateia

Gate of Rhegium

Column of Marcianus

Middle St.

Aqueduct

Golden Horn

Amastrianum

Cistern

Military Gate 3

Gate of the Pege or Selymbria

Forum of Arcadius

Forum of the Ox

Forum of Theodosius

Church of St. Mary of the Pege

Mesé (Middle St.)

Golden Gate

Military Gate 2

Gate of St. Aemilianus

Harbor of Theodosius

Gate of Kontoscalion

Gate of Psamathia

Church of John Baptist-Studion

Harbor of

Golden Gate

Church of St. Diomed

Sea of

Sycae

Bosporus

Horn

Gate of Drungarii

Gate of Perama   Harbor of Phosphorion   Chrysopolis

Gate of Neorion   Gate of St. Barbara

Gate of Eugenius

Column of Claudius

Acropolis   Kynegion

Imperial Basilica   Church of St. Eirene

Forum of   Middle St.   Church of St. Mary Hodegetria

Constantine   Ch. of   Church of St. Sophia

Church of   Anastasia   Augustaeum (Forum Area)

St. Thomas

Iron   Area of the Great Palace

Gate   Hippodrome   House of Justinian

Julian   Harbor of Hormisdas

Church of St. Sergius & St. Bacchus

Marmara

0   ¼   ½   1 mile

CONSTANTINOPLE

widely effective; and it was a program which could be finished in a limited space of time. The work could be done by a few men and it could be carried out in Constantinople itself under the Emperor's personal control. As a needed and welcome reform it would serve as a valuable means of showing the Emperor's intentions.

The ten men who formed the commission appointed to compile the new Code were given very wide powers. They were to omit anything that had become unnecessary or obsolete; to remove contradictions and repetitions; and to make such additions and even changes as were necessary. The commission included two men who were to play prominent roles in Justinian's future legislative undertakings, Tribonian, then a jurist in the civil service, and Theophilus, a professor of law in the University of Constantinople. The group worked with remarkable dispatch, and the new *Codex Iustinianus* was published in only a little over a year, on April 7, A.D. 529.

This Code, which put the administration of the law on a new basis, was a great achievement, but it was followed at once by an even more ambitious undertaking. This was the compilation of a digest of the jurisprudence of the great Roman lawyers of the second and third centuries, something that had never before been attempted on such a scale.

As the first step, it was necessary to resolve the considerable number of cases in which the classical jurists had been in disagreement on a given point. Each judge had been supposed to reconcile such disagreements for himself, as occasion arose, but the number of instances of conflict made the task time-consuming and sometimes uncertain. A collection entitled *Quinquaginta Decisiones* (Fifty Decisions) was made, representing the most important instances of dispute, with the correct decisions. This was published at the end of A.D. 530 or the beginning of A.D. 531.

When the compilation of the Fifty Decisions had been set on foot, it was possible to start work on the comprehensive Digest of Jurisprudence, and the order for this was issued on December 15, A.D. 530. This decree shows, characteristically, how Justinian was able to take advantage of the special talents of the men he found about him in Constantinople. What Tribonian's part had been in making the plan for the new Code we do not know. In the plan for the Digest, at least, he came into a major role. He had in the meantime been promoted to the post of Quæstor of the Sacred Palace, the highest legal office in the empire. His duties were to draft the laws which were issued in the Emperor's name, and also to prepare the Emperor's responses to petitions, a task which called not only for a profound knowledge of the law but a wide experience of affairs. Procopius, who disliked Tribonian, acknowledged that he had natural ability and a remarkably good education, and he was evidently a man of pleasing address. His career shows that he had a surpassing knowledge of the history of law, and he had made a collection of rare old books on the subject which were not to be found in the libraries.

Tribonian now indeed was made the leader of the enterprise. Moreover, he was to choose the members of the commission, a task of great responsibility even if the appointments had to be confirmed by the Emperor. He selected one high civil service official, four professors of law (two from the University of Constantinople, two from the imperial law school at Beyrouth), and eleven lawyers. One of the professors was Theophilus, of the University of

Constantinople, who had worked with Tribonian on the Code. The civil service official, Constantine, had also served on the commission for the Code.

Tribonian's commission was to read the works of the jurists of the earlier imperial period who had been empowered to make interpretations and give opinions. The best of this material was to be compiled and arranged. Obsolete or superfluous matter was to be omitted, contradictions and repetitions eliminated. Material already present in the new Code was to be used only when this was necessary for the sake of clarity. The commissioners had the power to abridge and alter texts. All this would make possible a tremendous improvement in the administration of the law.

The material was divided among three committees and the commission finished its task in December, A.D. 533. It had been expected that the work, *Digesta Iustiniani Augusti*, would take ten years, but it was completed in less than three. The commissioners had read 2,000 books, representing thirty-nine authors and containing three million lines, which they reduced to 150,000 lines. Many of the volumes used came from Tribonian's own library.

Since both law and jurisprudence were now collected and established, further commentary on the law was forbidden, in order to prevent the confusion which had made the Fifty Decisions and the Digest necessary. The Code and the Digest together represented the whole of the valid law, along with its interpretation—with the exception, of course, of such imperial legislation as might subsequently be issued.

One of his writings shows that Justinian had already been thinking of the requirements of the law schools in A.D. 530, and when work had been begun on the Digest, the need of new instructional material became urgent, for if commentary was to be forbidden in the future, there could be no privately prepared textbooks, and the existing manuals would become obsolete. To supply new material for the schools. Tribonian, while the Digest was being compiled, had work started on an introductory manual, the *Institutes*, which was to take the place of the classic manual of Gaius. Tribonian had the assistance of two professors of law, Theophilus of Constantinople, and Dorotheus of Beyrouth. The professors probably carried out the work under Tribonian's supervision. The new manual followed the commentaries of Gaius but brought them up to date and included new material dealing with Justinian's own legislation. The work was published on November 21, A.D. 533, and took effect, with the force of statute, on the same day as the Digest, December 30, A.D. 533.

At the same time the training of students was overhauled. In order to ensure better control of the instruction, the teaching of law was now to be permitted only at the two official schools, at Beyrouth and Constantinople, and the schools at Alexandria and Cæsarea were closed because the instruction given there had not been satisfactory. The four-year course was extended by making compulsory a fifth year, which had been optional. The first-year men had come to be called "Two-pounders," *dupondii*, no one quite knew why. Justinian thought this undignified and decreed that they should be called "Justinian's freshmen," *Iustiniani novi*. He also forbade hazing of freshmen.

This was the situation at the end of A.D. 533. It had now become plain that Justinian's original Code of April, A.D. 529 had already been rendered obsolete by the publication of the Fifty Decisions and of a large amount of new legislation; and Tribonian and his colleagues having demonstrated their remarkable skill and competence, an order was given, soon after the completion of the Digest for the compilation of a new Code. The work was to be done by Tribonian, Dorotheus of Beyrouth, and three lawyers, all of whom had been engaged on the Digest. As usual they were given wide powers of alteration and omission. The work was published on November 16, A.D. 534, to go into effect on December 29. This edition, which is extant, is divided into twelve books. Book 1 deals with ecclesiastical law; the sources of law; and the duties of higher officials. It is significant that ecclesiastical law here has the place of honor, which it had not had in the Code of Theodosius. Books 2–8 deal with private law, Book 9 with criminal law, Books 10–12 with administrative law. There are 4,652 laws in the collection.

Such was the result that had been achieved in only a little more than seven years after Justinian became emperor. New legislation, when it became necessary, was issued in the form of "New Constitutions," known as "Novels." Most of these dealt with ecclesiastical or public affairs. Some were concerned with points of private law over which doubt had arisen. Since commentary was forbidden, these doubts had to be referred to the Emperor himself for interpretation. In addition, there were new developments. The law of intestate succession was completely revised, and one very long Novel constitutes a code of Christian marriage law.

Justinian's constant endeavor to keep the law and its administration up to date is shown by the change in the language of the Novels. The Code, Digest, and Institutes were in Latin, the traditional language of the law, but this of course was not the natural language of judges, lawyers, or litigants in the eastern part of the empire. Latin was no longer currently spoken in Constantinople, though some members of the bureaucracy had to employ it, and some authors still wrote it. It was a considerable effort for the law students to learn Latin, and it had become unrealistic to carry on court proceedings in the language. Doubtless there was resistance to the change, but the Novels were composed in Greek—except, of course, when they were issued specifically for Latin speaking territories.

The new legislation both maintained the essential character of classical Roman law and adapted it where necessary to the changing needs of the society it had to serve. It was possible to preserve Roman law as a single system in the new Christian state because Constantine the Great had offered the Christians full membership in the state on the terms of Roman law. While a few modifications had to be made, it was possible to keep the body of the law unchanged in its main features. If Constantine had not taken the opportunity to incorporate the Christians in the state in this way, and if the action had not come solely from the side of the state, the character of the legal system would have been altered.

Legislation devised from the Christian point of view had already appeared in Constantine's time, and it was increasingly prominent in the work of Justinian. There was a real desire to make the laws more humane in some ways, in line with the current emphasis on the *philanthropia* or love toward mankind of the Emperor. The legal thought of Justinian's day shows a growing desire for equity as opposed to literal interpretation of strict laws. There is also a marked increase in the effort to protect persons who by their nature or position were weak against persons whose positions gave them power. Justinian's law for example favored the slave against the master, the debtor against the creditor, the ward against the guardian, the wife against the husband. There was also emerging the principle, little developed in classical times, that it is not right for a man to be enriched at the expense of another. At the same time certain penalties and punishments seem extraordinarily cruel; but they were not really excessive in relation to the habits of the day. Likewise the law preserved the old Roman concept of providing different punishments for the same offence, depending on whether the offender belonged to the upper classes or the lower classes.

If Justinian and some of his advisers were antiquarians, even archaizers in some respects, they did not perpetuate automatically all the concepts of the Roman legal structure. Certain Roman legal theories had never been popular in the Greek East, and local preferences, both Hellenistic and oriental in origin, were now brought within the system to replace Roman doctrine. This eastern influence appears most clearly in law concerning the family, inheritance, and dowry. The power of the father of the family, traditional in all Roman thinking, was weakened in the new legislation affecting the family. At the same time, the habits of mind developed by Greek philosophical training, which was at the heart of the contemporary educational system, can be seen in some of the classifications and reasoning in Justinian's legislation.

Finally, it is curious to see that the point of view inevitably developed in an autocratic state appears both in excessive regulation of human activities and in the belief that evil conditions, especially in the economy, can be done away with by legislation. This confidence in the efficaciousness of a decree goes back to Diocletian and Constantine, and was not a new feature of Justinian's law.

This immense legal accomplishment, surviving to form

the basis of European jurisprudence, far outlasted the Byzantine state. But its subsequent influence, now so much
better known, should not overshadow its effect in its own
day. By his revival and transformation of the law, Justinian
had strengthened the state and laid the foundation of future legislation. He had enormously enhanced, in this aspect, the prestige of the imperial office. The law was a kind
of personification of the imperial power, and the judge
was a direct personal representative of the Emperor. With
a newly authorized body of law came increased respect for
the Emperor. Ultimately, Justinian's work reminded his
people of the uniqueness of their legal inheritance and the
pride they might take in it. Roman law represented an
order and authority which did not exist among the barbarian peoples. This inheritance, saved and freshly set in
order by Justinian, could help build a worthy foundation
for the new Christian Roman Empire.

IV

THE ROMAN WORLD: *Reconquest*

THE STATUE of Justinian in the Augustæum, Procopius writes, showed the Emperor "stretching forth his right hand toward the rising sun, with fingers spread, commanding the barbarians in that quarter to remain at home and advance no further." The constant need for defense against the threat from the barbarians on the oriental frontier had been one of the reasons for the transfer of the capital to Constantinople, and this had become so much a major responsibility of the Emperor that it was included in the iconography of Justinian's statue. But balanced against the empire's success—more or less—in maintaining its eastern frontiers was the loss of the western territories, Britain, Gaul, Spain, North Africa, Italy. When the rule of the empire had been divided between two joint sovereigns, one in the East, the other in the West, its powers were already becoming unequal to the defense of the long borders. The eastern half of the empire proved stronger than the western, and was able to maintain itself; but in the last century before Justinian's time the western lands had fallen away one by one before the pressure of the Vandals and the Goths, the Germanic tribes which had forced themselves into the empire in two waves.

The Vandals had been able to come in by way of Gaul, then had occupied Spain, and finally had settled permanently in North Africa. Carthage was the Vandal capital. The Goths had conquered Italy and had set up a kingdom

there modelled on the Roman administration. Spain likewise was in the hands of the Goths. Gaul had been taken
over by other German tribes. Perhaps the greatest humilia-
tion of all, the most conspicuous sign of the empire's decline from its former greatness, had been the loss of Rome
itself. And it had not only fallen into the hands of the
barbarians; it had been pillaged so thoroughly by Alaric
and the Visigoths in A.D. 410, and then by the Vandals in
A.D. 455, that it had become a kind of empty monument,
all the sadder because the capital of Italy had been moved
to Ravenna.

So it was that the Mediterranean was no longer *mare
nostrum*, "Our Sea," as it had been to the Romans for centuries. At the time, the bitter loss of the western lands had
had to be accepted in Constantinople, and—as the statue in
the Augustæum indicated—it now seemed as though the
defense of the empire must be concentrated on the Mesopotamian border, for the Persians were growing in strength.
Conservative thinkers in Constantinople, at the time Justinian came to the throne, did not believe that the military
resources of the empire would be equal to anything more.

It was one of the traditional duties of the emperor to
guard and hand on the territories he had received, but this
would not content Justinian. If the empire was to be restored to its ancient place in the world, recovery of the
western provinces—or at least as much of them as could
be won back—was indispensable. The concept of one single, indivisible imperial unity still ruled men's minds, and
Justinian, of all men, was susceptible to this idea. Moreover, the loss of commerce in the western Mediterranean,
now in the hands of the barbarians, had been a severe blow
to the empire's prosperity. Recovery of these markets
would mean a great deal. The food supplies that could be

obtained from the fertile lands of North Africa would be a welcome addition to the rather limited production of the eastern Mediterranean.

The paramount consideration in any such plan was the question whether the army would be capable of carrying out its part. The composition of the Roman army in Justinian's day reflected the changes which had been taking place in the empire. The decline in the population had materially decreased the manpower available for military service, and it was no longer possible to find within the empire's borders all the men needed. Non-Roman allies and barbarian mercenaries had to be employed extensively, and foreign soldiers had sometimes found their way into the whole military force. Some foreigners rose to the highest commands, where they were able to influence imperial policy.

At the same time, the character of the army had been progressively changed to meet the new situation. The army had been divided into two different types of forces, the frontier garrison troops who were permanently settled on lands along the borders, and the mobile field army, composed of several different types of troops, which could be sent on expeditions as needed.

The frontier troops were a kind of militia, living on the land as farmers. They were the largest element in the army numerically, but their military value declined continually, in part because they were subject to economic exploitation by their commanders. They were much less well trained and less efficient than the members of the mobile forces, and were correspondingly less respected.

The field army had itself been changing in composition since the time when it had enjoyed its greatest development, under Constantine the Great. Its members were recruited in the provinces, especially Illyricum, Thrace, and Isauria. The recruits differed very much in their aptitude for military service. The best men came from Isauria, the wild mountain region in the southern part of Anatolia. The Isaurians were remarkable fighters, courageous and daring.

In the time of Justinian two further elements of the field army were becoming more important. One was the "Federates," a cavalry force composed of both citizens of the empire and peoples drawn from the nations around the borders. Organized and trained along Roman lines, these troops were the most efficient single component in the army. Along with them there served another class of cavalry called "Allies," barbarians such as Huns and Herulians whose princes had made treaties with the empire by which these units were supplied in return for money paid to the princes, or the use of land. The "Allies" were led by their native chiefs and were not always amenable to Roman military discipline, but they were expert horsemen and good fighters, and highly valuable as scouts.

Another component, irregular but of real importance, was the personal bodyguards of the generals. These guards were recruited and paid by the generals themselves, who furnished their equipment and saw to their training. They took an oath of loyalty to the Emperor, but they inevitably had a close personal allegiance to their employers. They were crack troops, proud of being selected for difficult and dangerous service, and in battle they were often reserved for use at the most critical points. Generals could become wealthy from their shares of the enemy spoils, and they were sometimes able to keep bodyguards of considerable size. Belisarius, Justinian's greatest general, who became very rich, at one time maintained 7,000 bodyguards.`

There was, finally the Emperor's bodyguard, which remained in Constantinople (unless the emperor went on a campaign himself) performing ceremonial duties in the palace. At the time he became emperor, Justin was commander of one of the regiments of imperial guards, and his nephew Justinian was a member of the guard.

In Justinian's day the army was efficient, if small numerically. An army which for centuries had had to deal with a succession of new enemies had had to learn how to profit from its lessons in battle. The enemy's mode of fighting was carefully studied, and improvements in weapons and tactics were regularly made. On the basis of experience with the barbarians, the cavalry had been developed until it became the chief component of the army in the sixth century. The heavy cavalry, in which both horse and rider wore armor, was one of the army's most effective striking forces. The superiority of the Persians' archery had taught the Romans the value of the bow, and the Roman archers on foot, with better weapons and training, were now superior to the Persians. Both the light and the heavy cavalry were armed with the bow, in addition to the lance and the sword, and this made the light cavalry especially valuable as a rapid striking force.

The total strength of the army in Justinian's reign was about 150,000. An expeditionary force usually numbered about 15,000, though it sometimes might grow to 25,000; but a field army of 40,000 was exceptionally large. Such armies often had to meet enemy forces which were much larger, but the Romans, unless severely handicapped, could always feel confident that they were superior to the barbarians in weapons, training, and discipline.

The available resources did not make it possible to raise a larger army, and the government now had established a policy of dealing with the barbarians by diplomatic means wherever possible. Money payments in the form of subsidies or annual tribute were often considered preferable to war. Because of its small size, and the expense of operation, the army was employed only as an extension of diplomatic action, and generals always had to avoid losses as much as possible.

If Justinian were to embark on the reconquest of the lost provinces, these were the instruments he would have to use. Many of his advisers considered that the army was only adequate for its existing duties in the eastern part of the empire, and that the dispatch of any expeditionary force to the West would only draw off troops who were badly needed in the East. Indeed many people in Constantinople thought the Emperor's scheme unwise. But Justinian was determined to go through with his plan, which none of his immediate predecessors had dared to attempt. He could not, however, put this program into effect soon after his accession, as he had done with the codification of the law; the reconquest was not a limited domestic program, but depended on both planning and opportunity.

In the existing conditions, a campaign in the West could be launched only if the Persian front were at least temporarily secure. This condition developed four years after Justinian came to the throne. A war had broken out with Persia in A.D. 502, in the reign of Anastasius, and this had ended in a truce in A.D. 505. Another war had begun just before the death of Justin, when the Persians threatened Roman interests in the border lands east of Anatolia. Justinian had to continue this war, but the fighting was ended when a new king came to the Persian throne in September, A.D. 531, and in the following year a treaty, known as the "Endless Peace," was made.

CONSTANTINOPLE

The accession of the new Persian ruler had coincided with a revolution among the Vandals in Carthage, in A.D. 531, and Justinian saw in this an opportunity for intervention in Africa. When the peace with Persia was made, troops could be withdrawn from that frontier, and their absence could be partly compensated by a major program of enlarging and improving the fortifications all along the eastern front. This construction program was begun immediately. Justinian was also encouraged by the emergence of a young general of notable talents, Belisarius, who had proved his ability during the recent Persian campaigns. One of the sources of Justinian's success was his ability to pick the best men available to carry out his projects. Having watched Belisarius' career, the Emperor saw that he was better qualified than any other general to lead an expedition to Africa, and that he could be entrusted with the extraordinary powers which the commander of such a distant expedition would have to have. In Belisarius, as in Tribonian, Justinian found a man who was eminently fitted to lead one of his great undertakings. The Emperor's choice was amply justified, for Belisarius became one of the great generals not only of his own day but of all time. He gave Justinian many years of faithful service, and it was primarily thanks to him that Africa and Italy were recovered.

The African expedition sailed from Constantinople in the third week of June, A.D. 533. The preparations must have been on a scale such as the city had never before witnessed. There were 16,000 fighting men, in addition to the services of supply. Ten thousand were infantry of the mobile army, the remainder cavalry. Three thousand of the cavalry came from the mobile army, 2,000 were Belisarius' private bodyguard, and there were 1,000 mounted archers from the Allies, made up of 600 Huns and 400

Herulians. A fleet of 500 transports of all sizes had been assembled, manned by 30,000 sailors from Egypt and from the coasts of Anatolia. The transports were protected by 92 warships, vessels with sails and single banks of oars, with decks to protect the oarsmen. Armed with rams, these warships were highly maneuverable and were capable of considerable speed, both cruising and fighting. Their crews, 2,000 men in all, were trained both to work the ships and to fight. When the fleet was ready, the General's flagship was brought to anchor off the promontory on which the Great Palace stood, and the expedition was blessed by the Patriarch Epiphanius.

The undertaking was a spectacular success, partly because of the efficiency of the Roman army and the skill of Belisarius' leadership, partly also because of the weakness of the Vandals. In one campaign of a few months the Vandals were defeated, their cities taken, and their king captured, along with all the royal treasure, which included the spoils carried away from Rome by the Vandals in A.D. 455. Belisarius returned to Constantinople in the summer of A.D. 534, just one year after he had left it.

The prompt recovery of Africa was such an auspicious opening of the reconquest that some especially significant way of celebrating it must be found. It had been a long while since the empire had enjoyed such a victory, and there were tangible evidences of the triumph—the captured king and the royal treasure—which would make an impressive exhibition. Also, of course, the results of the campaign were highly gratifying to the Emperor as a reply to the critics who had advised against it.

Here, then, was an occasion which offered Justinian a matchless opportunity to display the imperial power in terms of the image of the supreme Roman sovereign which he was trying to shape. Moreover, the people must be associated in some way with the imperial victory. This victory, a manifestation of Divine favor, was a victory of the whole empire, led by the Emperor and executed by his loyal army and people. In the commemoration of any such event, Constantinople itself would play an essential role as the capital, personifying the empire. Here the victory could be exhibited against the physical setting of the elements which formed the empire and made the victory possible.

The details of the celebration, as Justinian planned it, show the care with which all the potentialities of the occasion were developed. Ancient Roman tradition provided a precedent in the ceremony of the "triumph," a procession of thanksgiving in which the captives and the spoils were exhibited. In republican days in Rome, this procession had been led by the victorious general, riding in a chariot to the Capitolium, where he gave thanks in the temple of Jupiter Optimus Maximus, the special guardian of Rome. Under the empire, it was the emperor who led the procession, since the victory had been won in his name.

Some such procession was obviously called for now, but Justinian rearranged the details to suit the new concept of the Christian Roman emperor. He did not, on this occasion, follow the old custom of leading the procession himself. Instead, he decided to go back to the pre-imperial period, in which the general had led the parade. This had not been done for almost six hundred years, but the honor was now accorded to Belisarius. This arrangement not only had its antiquarian interest, and did honor to the general, but it preserved the role of the Emperor as Justinian conceived it, for it meant that Belisarius led the procession through the streets of Constantinople and then presented

the captives and the spoils to the Emperor in the Hippodrome. Justinian added another antiquarian touch. Cus-
tomarily, the general or emperor celebrating a triumph had
ridden in a chariot, or sometimes, at a later period, on
horseback. Here a significant change of detail was made.
This time, Belisarius walked on foot at the head of the
procession, setting out from his own house. This had been
the custom of the old Roman "ovation," a minor form of
triumph, which sometimes had been celebrated when a
full scale ceremony was not appropriate. Justinian's alteration was a very subtle one. The honor paid to Belisarius
was still very great; but it was not quite the honor that
it would have been to ride on horseback, or in a chariot.

Justinian also was able to make use of another tradition
which offered a permanent souvenir of the victory. It had
been the custom, both in the imperial period and earlier,
to issue heavy gold medallions, resembling coins but larger,
to commemorate noteworthy public events, such as a victory, a treaty with a foreign power, the anniversary of the
founding of Rome, or the anniversary of the emperor's
accession. These medallions were presented by the emperor to distinguished persons. Bearing appropriate in-
scriptions ("The Glory of the Romans," "The Safety of
the State," and so on), the medallions were excellent vehicles of propaganda for the regime. The Vandal victory
gave Justinian a welcome opportunity to add a new medal-
lion to the long and distinguished series of commemorative
pieces of his predecessors. A handsome medal was struck,
over three inches in diameter and half a Roman pound in
weight, showing the Emperor in full armor, on horseback,
carrying a spear, and preceded by the traditional figure of a
winged Victory.

The triumphal procession itself, as Procopius describes

it, must have been one of the most remarkable spectacles ever seen in Constantinople. First there was the loot taken from the palaces in Rome by the Vandals 79 years before—golden thrones, carriages; jewelry of all kinds, gold dinner services, plus, Procopius says, thousands of pounds of silver. Then there was the treasure of the Jews which Titus had taken to Rome after the capture of Jerusalem in A.D. 70. The Vandals had found this treasure in Rome and had taken it to Africa. It was now displayed in the procession—all the gold vessels which King Solomon had presented to the Temple in Jerusalem. After the triumph, the Emperor had these pieces sent to the Christian churches in Jerusalem.

After the treasure came the captives. The Vandals were objects of considerable interest in Constantinople because of their tall, well-made figures and blond coloring. The best looking prisoners had been selected to appear in the procession, along with King Gelimer and his family. The king, wearing a royal purple robe, was led before the Emperor's box in the Hippodrome, the robe was removed, and he was forced to prostrate himself before Justinian and Theodora. As a sign of his loyalty, Belisarius also did obeisance.

Magnanimity was *par excellence* an imperial virtue, and the Emperor could afford to be generous. After the triumph Gelimer was treated kindly and was held in honorable confinement on a country estate for the rest of his life. Characteristically, Justinian commanded to be made, for use in the palace, a gold table service decorated with scenes from his triumphs. The Emperor could be satisfied. Seven years after he had come to the throne the first part of his plan for the recovery of the lost provinces had been brilliantly accomplished, the spoils of Rome had been redeemed, and the king of a powerful barbarian nation had been humiliated before him and his people in the Hippodrome. This same year would see the completion of his codification of the law. Justinian was indeed on the way to making the Roman emperor once more a sovereign incomparably greater than any ruler on earth.

V

THE EMPEROR AS BUILDER: *St. Sophia*

IN HIS STATUE in the Augustæum, Justinian was portrayed in the midst of magnificent buildings he had constructed—the Church of St. Sophia, the entrance to the Great Palace, the Senate House. From the dome of St. Sophia one could have seen buildings everywhere in Constantinople and its environs that represented the Emperor's munificence.

The ruler as builder was one of the oldest concepts of the sovereign. Public buildings were at the same time generous gifts for the use of the ruler's subjects and enduring memorials of the ruler's name. The money used to build them often came from revenue supplied by the subjects, and the buildings were needed for public life; but even so the provision of buildings and public works of all kinds became one of the most admired official duties of the Roman emperor. Some rulers—Augustus, Trajan, Antoninus Pius, Diocletian, Constantine the Great, for example—were more active than others. The most fortunate were those like Constantine for whom a whole city filled with new buildings could be named. Constantinople, "The City of Constantine," was a permanent memorial of one of the most magnificent acts a ruler could perform, the establishment of a new capital of the empire and the construction of the essential buildings it needed to function as a capital. If the cost was a dangerous drain on the finances of the state, that was another matter. The emperor was bound to fulfil his function of providing public buildings and churches to serve as symbols of his reign.

Among the cities of the empire, the capital would naturally be the one to which the finest buildings would be given. Rome had become, through its monuments, an epitome of Roman history and a memorial of the Roman achievement. Athens in the same way preserved in its buildings the memory of Hellenic civilization. Constantinople was now the city which had been created to be the physical exemplar of the civilization of the Christian Roman Empire.

It would in any case have been Justinian's ambition to leave monuments worthy of his name in his capital. But circumstances gave him greater scope than an emperor could ordinarily expect for this side of his program. The Emperor Anastasius, while he had accumulated the considerable cash reserve which he left in the Treasury, had inevitably practised economies in the upkeep of public buildings, among other things, and when Justinian became emperor he found a more than normal need for repairs and replacements. Also the fires which occurred during the Nika Revolt in A.D. 532 made it necessary to replace several major public buildings and churches.

During his uncle's reign Justinian had already set about the rehabilitation or rebuilding of a number of churches in Constantinople and its suburbs. This work, which he began in a private capacity—many devout citizens gave their money for such purposes—was concerned with a special group of churches, the shrines of the early martyrs of Byzantium and the territory around it. Some of these had been built by Constantine the Great in recognition of the special honor which throughout the Christian world was paid to local saints. Justinian's early interest in these churches reflected the piety which was to show itself so clearly in his acts as emperor.

The chief church in this group was the shrine of St. Acacius, a Cappadocian soldier who had been executed at Byzantium in the early 300's and was venerated as one of the leading martyrs who had suffered on the site of the future Constantinople. This church, of the basilica plan popular in Constantine's time, had fallen into disrepair. Procopius describes the way in which it was rebuilt with columns and pavement both of dazzling white marble which produced the strong effect of light within the building which the people of that day loved in their churches.

Six other churches were similarly rebuilt. One was the Church of St. Mocius, martyred at Byzantium under Diocletian. This was one of the most famous shrines in Constantinople. It was said to have been originally a temple of Zeus, which had been converted into a church by Constantine the Great because it was the scene of the martyr's execution. The body of St. Mocius had been recovered and was buried there. Other churches in the city which were restored were those of St. Plato, martyred at Ancyra in the middle of the third century, and of St. Thyrsus, executed at Nicomedia in the same persecution. In the suburbs Justinian rebuilt one of the churches of the popular military saint, Theodore; a church of the famous woman martyr, St. Thecla, who suffered in the first Christian century; and the Church of St. Theodota, the mother who had been executed along with her children at Nicæa in the time of Diocletian.

When Justinian came to the throne, these private undertakings in the capital were replaced by an official program on a vast scale, which was a part of a great building program which extended through the whole empire. The reign of a man like Justinian would have been considered incomplete, by the people and by the Emperor himself, if it had not brought with it new monuments to the glory of the empire, and Justinian was eager to have a permanent literary record made of his buildings—for literature was more enduring than stone, and it was in the works of historians that an emperor's true fame would be preserved. Justinian was fortunate in having at his disposal the talents of the historian Procopius, and so it is that we have the panegyrical treatise *On the Buildings of the Emperor Justinian* which Procopius wrote, at the Emperor's command, in the years 559–560. The first part of the work is a special account of the buildings at Constantinople, composed as a spoken panegyric and delivered in the presence of the Emperor and his Court. The remainder of the book enumerates Justinian's buildings in the remainder of the empire.

Building programs such as Justinian undertook might sometimes really be only displays of wealth or signs of megalomania. But this was far from the case with Justinian. The record of his work at Constantinople shows that this was a balanced plan, designed for two purposes, first, to provide the people of the capital with needed public buildings and public works, and second, to create new and special architectural settings for the institutions which represented the chief resources, spiritual and political, of the empire and its civilization. Justinian surpassed the work of Constantine, who had been the greatest builder among the Christian emperors, and in one of his creations, the Church of St. Sophia, he produced the greatest church then existing in the world, which still stands as an example of what Constantinople must have been like during this spacious and splendid age.

Some of Justinian's public buildings represented continuing responsibilities of the state. Prominent in the lists of his works were free hospitals. One of the Emperor's best known benefactions was the rebuilding of a hospital for poor people which had been constructed in the early days of Constantinople by a private benefactor named Samson. Standing between the Church of St. Eirene and the Church of St. Sophia, this hospital had been burned during the Nika Riot. The Emperor now rebuilt and enlarged it, and increased the number of rooms. He also presented an endowment for the maintenance of the establishment. Such endowments of public institutions usually consisted of farm land or business property, the profits forming the income of the institution.

Other hospitals in and near Constantinople were also aided. Well outside the city, at a place called Argyronium, on the shore of the Bosporus as one sailed toward the Euxine Sea, there had been a free hospital for poor persons with incurable diseases. This had been neglected, and was rebuilt. Procopius mentions three other hospitals reconstructed by the Emperor and Empress, acting together. Justinian also constructed one of the free public guest houses which the government found it necessary to provide for the accommodation of poor people who came to Constantinople on business with the government.

Work was also done for the water supply which in a city like Constantinople needed constant maintenance. Regular upkeep was needed for the channels and public fountains; but the most important and most difficult problem was to maintain an adequate supply of water the year round. During the winter, which was the rainy season, the springs inside and outside the city produced more water than was needed at the time, and rain water was collected in open cisterns. The surplus, if not used, would have to be allowed to run off. In the summer, however, no rain fell and the springs did not give enough water for the city's current needs, always greater in hot weather. To equalize the supply, cisterns were built throughout the city, in which the surplus water of the winter could be stored for summer use.

In Justinian's time it was found that new storage was needed in the vicinity of the Augustæum. This presented a difficulty since this part of the city was densely built up and room for a new cistern would be hard to find. The problem was solved by excavating the large open court of the Imperial Basilica, west of St. Sophia, which contained the law library and was the headquarters for much of the judicial work of the government. The colonnaded court at the entrance to the basilica offered an open space of suitable dimensions. The pavement was taken up, and the portico along the southern side of the court was removed. A cistern was dug in the rock and when it was completed it was covered with a roof, supported on columns, which formed the new pavement of the courtyard.

In the same region there was general repair and improvement of the covered colonnades which lined the main street leading from the Augustæum to the Forum of Constantine. The public bath named for Zeuxippus was also embellished. In Justinian's day this bath, going back to the Roman period of Byzantium, was one of the show places of the city, with its collection of eighty classical statues, which were described by poets and copied by artists.

In the suburbs, a general program of development was carried out at Hebdomon, on the shore of the Sea of Marmara southwest of the city. A market place, public baths, and colonnades—some of the chief needs of municipal life— were built. The principal improvement was the construction of a sheltered harbor which would be of great value in this location. There were already two artificial harbors on the southern shore of the city itself, the Harbor of Julian and the Harbor of Theodosius, named for the emperors who had built them. These were enclosed by breakwaters and were used in the winter if the winds were blowing south through the Bosporus, making it impossible for ships coming up from the Sea of Marmara to get round the promontory and into the Golden Horn. The new harbor at the Hebdomon added a third refuge in stormy weather. The port was made by building two breakwaters running out from the shore at oblique angles, forming a protected entrance where they came together. The foundations were prepared by sinking open wooden chests filled with stones. When these had been built up to the surface of the water, rocks were piled on top of them. A similar harbor was built opposite this, on the Asiatic shore.

Like everyone who lived in Constantinople, Justinian had a lively appreciation of the beauties of the city's shores and surrounding waters, and so much of his building was along the water that he was criticized for spending more money there than he should. Part of this work may have been done to please Theodora, who loved the waterside. One characteristic project of the Emperor's was the construction of a park connected with a public bath at a place outside the city called Arcadianæ, on the Sea of Marmara. Foundations were laid in the water and a stone-paved court was built out from the shore. This was a spacious area paved with marble and surrounded by roofed colonnades of marble. The whole was decorated with bronze and marble statues, and it made a fine sight when the sunlight first reached it in the early morning, and again when it was shaded in the afternoon. The park was delightfully cool with the breezes from the water, and people came there to walk about and enjoy the air and the view. The sea was deep enough at this point so that pleasure boats could pass by quite close to the shore, and could stop if they wished. In the court was a statue of Theodora standing on a column of porphyry. Presented by the city of Constantinople in gratitude for the Emperor's gift of the park, the monument was a graceful memorial to the Empress who was so fond of gardens by the water.

But while so much money was spent on undertakings for the use of the citizens, it was even more needful for the Emperor to devote some of his work to buildings which would embody the prestige of the imperial house and the government. Here too Justinian had begun his operations during his uncle's reign. There was a small palace by the sea, near the Great Palace, originally built for a Persian prince, Hormisdas, who had been a refugee at the court of Constantine the Great. Justinian rebuilt this for his own use while his uncle was on the throne, and later, when he had become Emperor, he extended the precincts of the Great Palace to include the House of Justinian, as it was called. Its ruins, still standing by the sea, give an idea of the elegance of such a residence, as well as its solid construction of stone and brick. On the ground level was a terrace built over the water. From this three spacious doors, each twelve feet high, with stone frames and delicately carved lintels, led into the palace. Above the doors rose the seven brick arches of a loggia which opened on balconies fifty feet above the water.

When he became emperor, Justinian enlarged the Great Palace and built the Bronze Gate, to serve as a vestibule leading to the Augustæum. The vaulted roof was decorated with mosaics recording the victories in Africa and

Italy, and the passageway contained statues of former emperors and empresses. Near the Bronze Gate, on the east side of the Augustæum, Justinian built a Senate House in the Roman style, with a colonnaded porch and statues on the roof.

Great as these building operations were, they still yielded in number and importance to the Emperor's churches. Here Justinian made his greatest architectural contribution. We have the names of thirty-four churches which the Emperor built or rebuilt in Constantinople. Every Christian city in those days required an ample number of churches; and it was fitting that there should be even more than the usual number in the capital.

The churches with which Justinian was concerned were dedicated to many members of the celestial hierarchy and to a number of saints and martyrs. In addition to the local martyrs whose churches he built or rebuilt while still a private citizen, there are associated with the Emperor's name St. Sophia (that is, the Church of Christ the Wisdom of God); St. Eirene (the Church of the Peace of God); four churches of the Virgin, to whom the Emperor had a particular devotion; one of St. Anna; four churches of the Archangel Michael, who had a special cult at Constantinople and was venerated as a wonder-worker; a Church of St. John the Baptist; one of all the Apostles and another of St. Peter and St. Paul; and churches of joint dedication, to St. Sergius and St. Bacchus; to St. Priscus and St. Nicholas; to St. Cosmas and St. Damian; to St. Menas and St. Menæus. Other churches were built by the Emperor for Sts. Anthimus, Eirene, Panteleëmon, Tryphon, Ia, Zoe, and Lawrence. The list of names illustrates the richness of the religious life of the city.

Architecturally, Justinian's churches in Constantinople

illustrate the final development of the characteristic conception of the church building which was to be typical of Greek Christianity. After the official recognition of Christianity, the first Christian churches to be built reflected the plan of the Roman public basilica, with its aisles leading to an apse containing the altar. There were still churches of this type in Constantinople when Justinian came to the throne. But this style went out of favor in the territory of Greek Christianity with the introduction of the building of square or cruciform plan designed around a central dome.

This was a concept of the church edifice which gave it both a liturgical function and a symbolical significance which were much more congenial than the basilica to the Greek religious mind, and it was in churches of this type that Justinian's architectural ambition reached its fullest realization and set the precedent for later builders.

Essentially, the church of this type was either a square or a cross surmounted by a central dome. The designs of these churches show that the builders studied carefully the possibilities offered by variations in plan and interior decoration, with a view to obtaining different kinds of effects and giving each building its own individual stamp within the general framework of the liturgical and devotional purpose of the building. The structure below the dome might be conceived as a cube or a cross with equal arms which could be inscribed geometrically within a cube. Occasionally there might be a cross with the lower member longer than the others. The octagonal plan was also developed.

The dome might stand alone over the center of the square, or over the intersection of the arms of the cross; or a great central dome might be accompanied by smaller domes built over the arms of the cross. But it was in the central dome that the significance of the plan lay. The dome unified the whole structure and brought all its areas and spaces together around one central focus. The hemisphere which rose above this central spot symbolized heaven. It was visible at least in part to all the worshippers in the church, and in this way it served to bind all the congregation together, during their worship, as one body of faithful. And the faithful, gathered under the dome, in a square, cruciform, or octagonal space, could see each other, and were much more aware of each other's presence than they could be in a basilica of the old type. The altar was usually placed in an apse in the east of the building, and in the square or cruciform plan the congregation was closer to the altar than they had been in churches of the elongated basilica plan. In some buildings, indeed, the altar now stood under the central dome, giving an even greater feeling of unity to the structure and the congregation.

Beyond all this, the dome created the impression of vast space, and gave the whole interior of the church a majesty and dignity which imparted a sense of peace and detachment. It was in these terms that the dome seemed to bring heaven to earth; and in this lofty vaulted space the worshipper could feel himself truly in touch with the communion of saints and the cloud of witnesses, and the community of the faithful on earth would seem very close to those who had gone before.

Restoring or enlarging old churches, and building new ones, Justinian had ample opportunity to employ all the devices of architecture and decoration to enrich the spiritual life of Constantinople and to make the churches of the capital an ideal for the rest of the empire. Here Justinian also sought to realize the function of architecture which of all art forms could set forth perhaps most clearly the many varieties of thought and feeling of the people for whom it was built. The Emperor did not by any means allow his churches to fall into a pattern of style and decoration. Built at different times, the leading examples of his work were all designed differently. In one case he built two churches side by side to illustrate different plans. These were the Church of St. Peter and St. Paul, and the Church of St. Sergius and St. Bacchus, built on the shore of the Sea of Marmara, near the Great Palace. Placed at right angles to one another and sharing the same entrance court, the Church of St. Peter and St. Paul was a basilica, while that of St. Sergius and St. Bacchus had had an octagonal interior. This church still exists in its picturesque setting near the sea wall. Attached to the Church of St. Sergius and St. Bacchus Justinian built a monastery for noblemen who wished to take vows and retire from the world.

Another of Justinian's churches is still standing, St. Eirene, a domed basilica near St. Sophia. This, like St. Sophia, replaced a church of Constantine the Great. It was the church used for daily services by the patriarch of Constantinople when he was not officiating on special occasions in St. Sophia or elsewhere.

The Church of the Holy Apostles—dedicated to all the apostles together—likewise replaced a building of Constantine the Great. Cruciform in plan, with a central dome plus smaller domes over each arm of the cross, this church was distinguished by having the altar in the center of the building, under the main dome. The Holy Apostles occupied a special place among the churches of the city. It had been intended by Constantine the Great as the burial place of his dynasty, and a mausoleum had been built, outside the apse of the church, for the reception of the imperial sarcophagi. Here lay the marble sarcophagus of Constantine surrounded by the tombs of the members of his family and his successors.

Under Constantine's sons, the Church of the Holy Apostles had taken on tremendous sanctity when it received the relics pronounced to be those of St. Andrew, St. Luke and St. Timothy, which were discovered in the 350's. The recovery and reburial of St. Andrew's remains was an event of singular importance, since it was by him, according to tradition, that Christianity had been brought to Byzantium. Buried beneath the altar, the relics of the three apostles gave the church a prestige of a kind that no other shrine in Constantinople possessed.

By Justinian's time, the mausoleum of Constantine had become full, and Justinian constructed a new tomb near it for himself and his successors. The Church of the Holy Apostles was regarded as second in importance after St. Sophia, and the Emperor and his court attended services which were held in it on a number of the major festivals of the church year. In the church calendar, the commemoration of St. Peter and St. Paul, the chiefs of the apostles, on June 29, was followed by the festival of all the apostles together on June 30, and on those days the church was the center of magnificent celebrations, with processions through the streets of the city. This church was so famous that its plan and construction were imitated by the builders of St. Mark's in Venice.

Taken all together, these shrines, with those built throughout the empire, would have given Justinian an enviable reputation as a builder of churches; but they were all surpassed by the Church of St. Sophia, which was often called simply "the Great Church," the title given to the principal

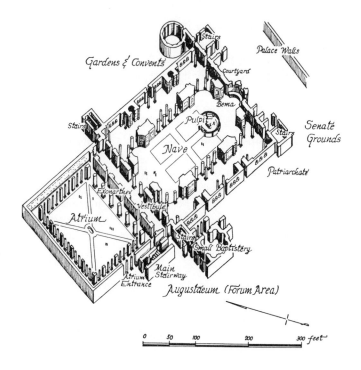

Justinian's Church of St. Sophia. Restoration of the Original Plan by Henri Prost

church in each large city. In St. Sophia Justinian created a church in which the mind could reach its noblest feelings, and it might well have been the building of this church that the Emperor would have regarded as his greatest achievement.

The thought of such a church was evidently in Justinian's mind from an early period. The existing Church of St. Sophia was burned on January 13, 532, in one of the devastating fires which broke out during the Nika Riot, and the construction of the new church was begun only forty days later, on February 23. Even if the plans for the new building could have been prepared in forty days, the idea must already have come to the Emperor before the fire unexpectedly gave him his opportunity. If the fire had not occurred, the existing church would in time have been torn down. The Nika Riot was also an unlooked for source of the funds used to build the church, which came in part from the confiscated estates of the senators who had been implicated in the rebellion.

It is one of the most characteristic indexes of the spiritual life of Constantinople in the days of Justinian that in the midst of so many churches dedicated to so many different members of the celestial hierarchy, the Emperor chose to build, as his own greatest church—which was intended to be the greatest church in the world—a shrine dedicated to Christ as *Hagia Sophia*, Holy Wisdom. Christ, the Wisdom *(sophia)* and Power*(dynamis)* of God, in St. Paul's words, represented the action of the second person of the Trinity among men. It is by no means mere chance that the chief temples of pagan Athens and Christian Constantinople were both dedicated to Wisdom. The Parthenon as the shrine of Athene, Goddess of Wisdom, and Justinian's church both show the respect for *sophia* which has ever been one of the chief traits of the Greek mind. Christ as the Wisdom of God was a familiar idea to Greek Christians; the Hymn of the Resurrection, sung during the Eucharist after the people have received the bread and wine, invokes Christ as "the Wisdom and the Word and Power of God." St. Sophia stood near, and was a kind of spiritual companion to, the Church of St. Eirene, representing the Peace of God, which had, like the original St. Sophia, been built by Constantine the Great. It is significant that when both St. Eirene and St. Sophia were burnt and rebuilt, it was Wisdom that was given first place.

For architects, Justinian was again fortunate. As he had found helpers of special talents for law and war in Tribonian and Belisarius, he also commanded the services of two builders of singular powers, Anthemius of Tralles and Isidorus of Miletus. Anthemius belonged to a family of distinguished physicians and lawyers. He and Isidorus were both noted mathematicians, as well as builders, and their mathematical abilities were of basic importance in the exacting task given them by Justinian.

St. Sophia could in fact have been executed only by builders of real skill. It was based on traditional Roman styles, and built in the traditional medium—the combination of stone with brick laid in thick beds of mortar, the surfaces faced with plaster or marble veneer. The architects and builders of the Græco-Roman world had long handled their material with skill and confidence, but St. Sophia represented a design and a scale that had never been attempted. The main area of the interior, designed for the services, was a great oval 250 feet by 107 feet; with the side aisles, the main floor made almost a square, 250 feet by 220 feet. The nave was covered by a dome 107 feet in diameter, rising 180 feet above the ground (the dome of the Church of St. Sergius and St. Bacchus, for example, was 69 feet 6 inches above the ground).

The design created the impression of a vast enclosed space, made possible by an intricate series of supports, all of which were arranged so as to lead the spectator's eye from the ground level up to the dome. At the east and west of the nave were hemicycles crowned by semi-domes, which provided some of the support for the superstructure; each hemicycle was flanked and supported by two semicircular exedras carrying smaller semidomes. At the eastern end the hemicycle opened into the apse with its semidome. With rows of columns supporting the upper galleries on the north and south of the nave, and numbers of clear windows in the walls, in the semidomes, and around the base of the main dome, the supporting elements looked incredibly slender and light. The ring of forty-two arched windows placed close side by side at the springing of the main dome seemed almost to separate the dome itself from the rest of the structure. Procopius in his account of the wonderful building tells of the astonishing effect of these details—the structural elements seemed to come together in mid air and float away from one another, each resting only on the part next to it. The weight of the upper part of the building appeared to be borne on terrifyingly inadequate supports, though of course it was very carefully braced. The dome itself, as Procopius said, seemed not to rest upon solid masonry at all; instead it appeared to be suspended by a golden chain from heaven. The bold conception and design of the building were matched by the skill with which it was constructed; but a structure of such size and such daring plan was never again attempted in Constantinople.

Just as the fabric of the building represented the desire

to produce a transcendent spiritual effect, the decoration was carefully studied toward the same end. Typically of Byzantine church architecture, applied ornament was concentrated in the interior, and the outside of the building was left plain, so as to show the mass of the structure, and bring out the lines of the building as it was put together out of the geometrical elements which the Byzantine mind so greatly appreciated. In all such church buildings, the combination of vertical lines and curves gave sufficient pleasure to the eye, and the plain masses made a striking effect in the bright sunlight of Constantinople.

In the interior the decoration was sumptuous but never risked being gaudy. It was planned with a richness which was only possible when the whole empire could be laid under contribution to furnish the materials. Paul the Silentiary, one of the members of Justinian's court, wrote an elaborate description of the church in verse which shows us what the magnificence of the decoration must have been when it was in its original state. Many lands, Paul says, sent their own characteristic marbles, each with its distinctive colors and veining. There were black stone from the Bosporus region, with white streaks; green marble from Carystus in Greece; polychrome stone from Phrygia; porphyry flecked with silver from Egypt; an emerald green marble from Sparta; an Isaurian marble with red and white veins; yellow stone from Libya, onyx, and other rare marbles. The different stones were used in carefully planned combinations in the columns, in the pavement, and in the revetment of the walls. The plaques were cut so as to take advantage of the patterns formed by the veins, and Paul the Silentiary compared the whole effect to meadows of flowers on the floor and walls.

Rising above was the great dome, showing the Cross outlined against a background of gold mosaic. The semidomes were also finished in gold mosaic, and the pendentives beneath the dome were filled with mosaic figures of seraphim, their wings like peacock feathers.

Against the background of the marbles and mosaics the church was filled with objects of shining metal, gold, silver, and brass. From the rim of the dome hung brass chains supporting innumerable oil lamps of silver, containing glass cups in which the burning wick floated in the oil. Beside the side colonnades which stretched the length of the church, separating the aisles from the nave, hung other rows of silver lamps. The capitals of the columns were bound with gilded bands of brass.

It was in the sanctuary, however, that the precious metals were used to their fullest effect. The visitor would first see the inconostasis, the columnar screen which stood in front of the altar. The screen itself was made of silver plated with gold. Depicted on it were Christ, the Virgin Mary, and the apostles. At intervals in front of the screen were lamp stands shaped like trees, broad at the base, tapering at the top. In the center of the screen, brightly illuminated, was the figure of the Cross. The gates leading into the sanctuary bore the monogram of Justinian and Theodora.

Within the sanctuary was the holy table, a slab of gold inlaid with precious stones, supported by four gold columns. Behind the altar, in the semicircular curve of the apse, were the seven seats of the priests and the throne of the patriarch, all of gilded silver. Over the altar hung a cone-shaped ciborium or canopy, with nielloed designs. Above the ciborium was a globe of solid gold, weighing 118 pounds, surmounted by a cross, inlaid with precious stones, which weighed 80 pounds. The eucharistic vessels—

chalices, patens, spoons, basins, ewers, fans—were all of solid gold set with precious stones and pearls, as were the candelabra and censers.

Around the altar hung red curtains bearing woven figures of Christ, flanked by St. Peter and St. Paul. Paul the Silentiary describes the scenes. Christ, the supremely commanding figure of Byzantine art, wore "a garment shimmering with gold, like the rays of the rosy-fingered dawn, which flashes down to the divine knees, and a chiton, deep red from the Tyrian shell dye, covers the right shoulder . . . The upper robe has slipped away and pulled up across the side it only covers the left shoulder while the forearm and the hand are bare. He seems to point the fingers of the right hand, as if preaching the Words of Life, and in the left hand he holds the Book of the Divine Message—the Book that tells what the Messiah accomplished when his foot was on the earth. And the whole robe shines with gold; for on it a thin gold thread is led through the web . . . And on either side stand the two messengers of God—Paul, full of divine wisdom, and also the mighty doorkeeper of the Gates of Heaven, binding with both heavenly and earthly chains. One holds the Book pregnant with sacred words, and the other the form of a cross on a staff of gold. The cunning web has clothed both in robes of silver white . . . On the borders of the curtain, indescribable art has figured the works of mercy of our City's rulers; here one sees hospitals for the sick, there sacred churches, while on either side are displayed the miracles of Christ . . . But on the other curtains you see the kings of the earth, on one side with their hands joined to those of the Virgin, on the other side joined to those of Christ, and all is cunningly wrought by the threads of the woof with the sheen of a golden warp . . ."

To the feeling of space and of regal splendor there was joined a third impression, that of light. If one entered it by day, the building seemed flooded by sunlight. Procopius wrote that the reflection of the sunlight from the marbles made one think that the church was not illuminated by the sun from without, but that the radiance came into being within the building. By night, the whole vast interior seemed filled with the light from the thousands of oil lamps, all hung at different levels, giving a brilliant illumination in which there were no shadows.

This sense of light completed the effect on the worshipper. Procopius puts this very finely: "Whenever anyone comes to the church to pray, he realizes at once that it is not by human power or skill, but by divine influence that this church has been so wonderfully built. His mind is lifted up on high to God, feeling that he cannot be far away but must love to dwell in this place he has chosen. And this does not happen only when one sees the church for the first time, but the same thing occurs to the visitor on each successive occasion, as if the sight were ever a new one. No one has ever had a surfeit of this spectacle, but when they are present in the building men rejoice in what they see, and when they are away from it, they take delight in talking of it."

Paul the Silentiary speaks more directly of the effect of the lamps. Whoever gazes on the lighted lamps of the iconostasis, Paul writes, "feels his heart warmed with joy; and looking on a lamp in the shape of a boat swathed with fire, or on some single lamp, or the symbol of the Divine Christ, all care vanishes from the mind, as when the wayfarer gazes on the stars of heaven . . . Thus through the spaces of the great church come rays of light, expelling clouds of care, and filling the mind with joy." With the light shining through its windows at night, the great church dominated the whole of Constantinople. Paul the Silentiary tells how the lighted building, rising above the dark mass of the promontory, cheered the sailors who saw it from their ships in the Bosporus or the Sea of Marmara; the church showed the way to travellers "as it also shows the way to the living God."

It took five years to complete St. Sophia. The tradition was that ten thousand workmen were engaged on the building, under the direction of one hundred foremen. Before it was completed, Justinian fixed the staff of the church at sixty priests, one hundred deacons, forty deaconesses, ninety subdeacons, and one hundred readers and twenty-five singers to assist in the services. There were one hundred custodians and porters.

The story of the dedication is that when the building was ready to be consecrated, the Emperor walked in procession from the gate of the palace across the Augustæum to the outer doors of the church. Preceded by the Cross, the Emperor and the Patriarch then entered the vestibule. Then the Emperor passed into the building alone and walked to the pulpit, where he stretched out his hands to heaven, and cried, "Glory be to God, who has thought me worthy to finish this work! Solomon, I have surpassed thee!" This account may perhaps be somewhat embroidered; but the words attributed to Justinian must have occurred to him—and to others—when the completed church was first opened.

VI

EMPIRE AND BODY OF CHRIST: *The Divine Liturgy*

IN THE AGE of Justinian, every step of human life was blessed, strengthened, and aided by the Church. The faithful were cared for from birth to death by the sacraments of Baptism, Confirmation, Confession, Holy Communion, Marriage, and Holy Unction (a healing service). Ordination formed the seventh sacrament. Other services watched over the believer's mundane affairs. There was, for example, a service for the blessing of a new house. Not only were there prayers to be said for a mother on the day on which a child was born, but there were prayers for the women who came to assist at the birth. There were services for those setting out on a journey, with special prayers for those about to travel by water.

The daily life of the Church itself centered about a series of services which marked the divisions and hours of the day. These began with the First Hour, the opening service of the morning, with thanksgiving for the light of the new day; the Third Hour (which at present would be about nine o'clock), commemorating the descent of the Holy Spirit at Pentecost; the Sixth Hour (noon), commemorating the Crucifixion of Christ; and the Ninth Hour (three in the afternoon), commemorating the death of Christ. The ordinary person was not usually able to take part in all these services, but they were celebrated daily by the priests and deacons in the churches, and by the monks and nuns in their communities.

But it was in the stated services of the cycle of the festivals of the church year that the corporate life of the Church was chiefly expressed. On each Sunday, as the anniversary of the Resurrection, there took place a celebration of the Divine Liturgy, the service of Holy Communion which was the primary service of worship of the Church. In addition, the calendar was filled, on both Sundays and week days, with the special services which constituted the Christian year. At each of these, the Divine Liturgy was celebrated, along with the particular service provided for the occasion.

The greatest festivals were of course those which commemorated the events in the life of Christ. Beginning with the Annunciation (March 25), the cycle continued with the Nativity (December 25), the Circumcision (January 1), which was also the feast of St. Basil the Great; and the Manifestation of God, or Epiphany (January 6). After the special services of Lent, Palm Sunday inaugurated Holy Week, during which special services were held each day, leading up to Good Friday and then to Easter Sunday, the greatest festival of the Church. There followed the Ascension, and Pentecost. The Transfiguration fell on August 6.

The events in the Life of the Virgin Mary were also commemorated on the appropriate days. Other great festivals were the Blessing of the Waters, at Epiphany (January 6), the Discovery of the Holy Cross (August 1), and the Exaltation of the Precious and Life-Giving Cross (September 14).

In addition, all through the year came the commemorations of the apostles, martyrs and saints—all the servants of the Church who by their lives and deaths had earned a glorious memory which their successors in the company of the faithful kept alive by annual festivals. Each commemoration was fixed on the saint's day of death or martyrdom, or on the anniversary of some other event of significance in his life, such as the Conversion of St. Paul (January 25). Often several anniversaries fell on the same day.

In Constantinople, May was a notable month, with festivals on the eleventh, the anniversary of the founding of the city by Constantine the Great, and on the twenty-first, the day devoted to St. Constantine the Great and his mother, the pious St. Helena. Two local martyrs had their festivals in this month, St. Acacius on the eighth, and St. Mocius on the eleventh. On these days the special services were held in the churches in honor of these martyrs which had been built by Constantine and rebuilt by Justinian. At the end of June, Justinian's new Church of the Holy Apostles was the scene of special festival services on the days devoted to St. Peter and St. Paul (twenty-ninth) and to all the apostles (thirtieth). Other important festivals in Constantinople were the anniversaries of more local martyrs, such as St. Theodota (September 2), St. Plato (November 18), and St. Thyrsus (December 14).

But paramount among all these services was the Divine Liturgy; and in Constantinople the most important place of its celebration was St. Sophia, the imperial church which the sovereign and his court attended on many of the major days of the church year. The Emperor was present there at the services of Christmas, Epiphany, Good Friday, Easter Monday, the Sunday after Easter, Pentecost, the Exaltation of the Cross, and a number of other festivals.

Around the altar of St. Sophia, we are told, were inscribed these words: "We [Justinian and Theodora] thy servants, O Christ, bring to thee of thine own, praying that thou wilt graciously accept it, O Son and Word of God, made flesh and crucified for us. Strengthen us in the true faith, increase and guard this state which thou hast entrusted to us, through the mediation of Mary, the holy Virgin, the Mother of God."

The first part of the inscription was an echo of a passage in King David's hymn of thanksgiving, sung when he and his people made their offerings for the building of a temple of God: "But who am I, and what is my people, that we should be able to offer so willingly after this sort? for all things come of thee, and of thine own have we given thee." The use of the inscription of course implied a parallel between King David and the Emperor Justinian. These words expressed so well the Christian idea of offering to God that they were used in the service of the Holy Communion when the priest offered the gifts at the altar: "We bring before thee thine own, from thine own, in all things and for all things."

Chosen for inscription on the most sacred spot in the church, and spoken at every celebration of the Eucharist, these words were a perpetual reminder of the true function of this church dedicated to Christ. The church itself was an offering of the whole people—led by the Emperor as the builder—and its real purpose was to provide a new and glorious setting for the performance of the Divine Liturgy, the sacrifice of praise and thanksgiving. St. Sophia, incomparably splendid as it was, had not been created simply as a unique architectural monument or an artistic wonder. It had been planned, as a church of unparalleled richness and beauty, as a setting for the worship of God.

The performance of the liturgy was a corporate act of the whole congregation, acting as one portion of the larger Christian community. Religion and citizenship went together. To be a member of the Orthodox Church was to be a citizen of the empire, and to be a citizen was to be a Christian; and so participation in the Church's most important service of worship was at the same time an expression of social and political community. When the Emperor attended a service, as the leader of his people, the service became an occasion on which state and Church, people, clergy, and sovereign were united in their highest religious duty; and so it was fitting that the Emperor should provide a special church worthy of such a coming together—and worthy, at the same time, of the mystical presence of Christ and the Holy Spirit. And for Justinian, of course, it was necessary to build a shrine that would outdo everything that man had ever built. If all things come from above, the offering that is made in return should be the richest that can be made, both materially and spiritually, symbolizing the believer's offering of himself and of all that he possesses, and his finest creations. It is only thus that the believer can realize what wealth has been given to the world.

In the Constantinople of Justinian's time the text of the Divine Liturgy in common use was ascribed to St. John Chrysostom of Antioch, the "Golden Tongued," who had ended his career as Patriarch of Constantinople. Whether or not the service was really written by him, the beauty of the language was worthy of his name. It was an ample and unhurried service, never abbreviated. Normally it was preceded by the service of Matins; the two together would take three hours, sometimes more.

Greek Christianity, philosophical, speculative, mystical— and always literary—saw its prayers, hymns, and worship as an expression of its devotional thought in all the varied and subtle forms this thought might take. The nature of God and Christ, their attributes and their manifestations, had to be carefully and fully set forth in stately language, in which any attempt at brevity or conciseness would have meant possible loss of spiritual thought. The literary form must be worthy of the spiritual experience. In Greek Christianity, devotional thought took its start from the Scriptures, and everywhere in every service, almost in every prayer and hymn, the worshipper would hear some phrase which bound his thoughts to the sacred books. The Psalms and the New Testament were the writings most frequently quoted. In the rotation of the church calendar, the singing of the Psalms and the daily reading of selections from the Gospels and the Epistles kept all the members of the Church, priests and laity alike, constantly in touch with the biblical teachings which were the source of their faith. As the daily lessons progressed through the Scriptures, the special prayers and intercessions changed according to the day and the occasion of the service. The hymns likewise changed daily, and on each day of the week the music was sung in a special key.

Thus, if the services were elaborate, they were not static. They were long, but this was because there was much to be said and sung, and to omit any of this, or to curtail a service temporarily, would have been to lose something precious; the whole act of worship would be rendered vain. If the essential contents of the services were not changed, this did not mean that they were stagnant; it was simply that the texts were considered to be complete and perfect, wholly satisfying the need. They had reached a state which could not be bettered.

More than this, spiritual satisfaction, and spiritual strength, came from the performances of services with which earlier generations of Christians had worshipped. A great deal of the significance and the solidity of the faith lay in the fact that it bound together the Christians of the present and those of the past in the continuing life of the Church. Here the liturgy, with the other sacraments and all the other services, provided a continuity in which the individual Christian felt himself a part of the great living Body of Christ, in which were linked together the faithful on earth and those who had gone before.

In addition to the chronological link, running vertically down through history, there was also the geographical bond, spreading horizontally through the empire. The Divine Liturgy was the same everywhere. The same words, whether in Greek, Syriac or Coptic, would be said or sung in the humblest village in Syria or Egypt, and in St. Sophia. The bread and the wine, the Body and Blood of Christ, might be mixed in a bronze bowl in a little country church in Anatolia, and in the magnificent gold chalice studded with jewels in St. Sophia; the prayers were the same, and the bread and wine were offered to all believers. Moreover, it was of the utmost significance that if necessary the liturgy was translated from Greek and celebrated in the local language. This use of the language of the communicant was of enormous importance not only in the religious life of the empire, but in the religious and political histories of the barbarian nations.

The setting too could play its part. It was not simply because it was the imperial church in the capital of the empire that St. Sophia celebrated the Divine Liturgy with all the splendor that could be devised. The very size of the building, the magnificence of the marbles and mosaics, the crowd of silver lamps, the gold and jewels of the altar, the glittering vestments of the clergy and the gorgeous robes of the imperial court, the incense—all this was not merely a display of wealth and power, considered suitable to the church in which the Emperor worshipped. Nor was the splendor of the services in other great cities of the empire merely a display of local wealth, or of the power and magnificence of the bishop. The ceremony was not a tactless contrast to the humility and poverty of the earthly life of Christ. The service was magnificent—as magnificent as it was possible to make it—because of its tremendous implications. It must be a setting for the Kingship of Christ and for the commemoration of the Last Supper, the Crucifixion and the Resurrection, by which Christ had showed himself to be Lord of lords and King of kings. During the liturgy, Christ's people prayed that he come into the church, "invisibly escorted by the angelic hosts." The church must be worthy of this mystical presence.

The physical splendor of the ceremony filled the worshipper's eye and helped him feel the magnificence of the physical offering that was being made. Another effect came from the music, as a living creation which was an integral part of the service. Music—unaccompanied singing, for instrumental music was felt to be worldly and was only used on secular occasions—had always played a part in Christian worship. In Justinian's day the music of the Church was going through a major transformation which greatly enhanced the beauty and significance of the sung parts of the service. This change had come about through the development of rhythmical poetry, which had begun to supplant the classical forms based on the quantity of the vowels. The new rhythmic style corresponded to changes which had been taking place in the spoken language, and the hymns and religious poems which began to be written in the time of Justinian had a much greater appeal to the congregations. The leading poet of the new style, Romanus, a gifted Syrian deacon, had come to live in Constantinople in the time of the Emperor Anastasius. He produced an enormous collection of poems and hymns for all occasions in the Christian year and all parts of the services, and the quantity of his writings—he was said to have written one thousand hymns—shows that there was a real response to his style. The Emperor Justinian himself was said to have composed a hymn on "Christ the Only-Begotten Son" which was in regular use. As these hymns were sung by the choirs, the voices of the men and boys, rising through the whole service in hymns and responses, would fill the church with musical praise which, to the listening congregation, might seem to lift the whole building up above the earth.

Preparation for participation in the Divine Liturgy began the day before, with the confession and absolution of each person who desired to receive communion. There followed an evening service for the preparation of the communicants. Here there were a number of beautiful prayers, attributed to St. Basil the Great and St. John Chrysostom, in which the person intending to receive communion confessed his faults and prayed for cleansing and enlightenment. In one of these prayers there appears a characteristic motif which recurs throughout the liturgy, namely the thought of the unity and the continuity of the Church, in this life and beyond:

> Be thou my helper and defender, sustain my life in peace, and count me worthy of a place among thy saints at thy right hand, through the prayers of all the saints which have been pleasing to thee since the world began.

In the early morning, Matins were celebrated, and after this, without a break, the Divine Liturgy began with the preliminary service of the vesting of the clergy and the preparation of the bread and wine. In a great church such as St. Sophia, the chief celebrant might be a priest of the church's staff, but on great occasions he would be a bishop or the Patriarch of Constantinople himself. A distinguished ecclesiastic visiting the city might be invited to celebrate. During his performance of the rites, a group of priests or bishops would attend the celebrant as a mark of honor and respect, and at a great festival, at which the Emperor would be present, the sanctuary and the space before it would be filled with dignitaries in their rich robes.

The preliminary service opened with the characteristic phrase, spoken by the priest, "Blessed is our God, now and for ever and world without end." These words were used at the beginning of many services; they had the effect of starting the rite with a theme that was to run all through it. In the initial prayers, the ministers prayed to be made worthy of their task. They then went into the sanctuary through the doors of the iconostasis, and the celebrant began his vesting. He was already wearing an ankle-length tunic with tight wrist-length sleeves. Over this, with the assistance of the deacon, he placed the special vestments worn during the Liturgy—the dalmatic, a robe with long loose sleeves, and over this the chasuble, something like a sleeveless cloak.

The priest then washed his hands and approached the table on which the bread and wine had been set out. The bread was leavened, in the form of round loaves, stamped with the cross on one side. Five loaves were provided, and the celebrant cut particles out of each of them, representing the Virgin Mary, John the Baptist, the prophets, apostles, and other figures. The particles were set on the paten in a fixed symbolic order. Then the celebrant, taking the censer filled with burning incense from the deacon, censed the bread, and then the chalice, in which the deacon had put wine and water. All these actions were accompanied by prayers. The deacon then censed the whole sanctuary, the altar, and the celebrant, and went out and censed the people in the nave. After this the celebrant kissed the Book of the Gospels which was lying on the altar, and it was time to begin the Divine Liturgy itself.

The liturgy opened with a rather more elaborate blessing pronounced by the celebrant, "Blessed be the Kingdom of the Father and of the Son and of the Holy Ghost, now and for ever and from all ages to all ages." There followed a set of prayers for peace and salvation, said by the deacon, with responses sung by the choir. After these came a series of antiphonal anthems and prayers.

The celebrant and the deacon then entered the sanctuary, took the richly bound Gospel book from the altar, and carried it through the church and again into the sanctuary. There followed hymns for the day and then the appointed lessons for the day, first from the Acts or Epistles, then from the Gospels.

Between the reading of the Epistle and the Gospel the priest said a prayer for knowledge which shows very typically the stress which the Greeks of all periods—from Plato to Justinian—placed on wisdom and learning as the means by which man may seek "a heavenly citizenship":

O Merciful Master, cause the pure light of the knowledge of thee to shine in our hearts, and open the eyes of our mind to perceive thy message of Good Tidings; fill us with the fear of thy blessed commandments, that we, trampling down our fleshly desires, may seek a heavenly citizenship, and may do and consider all those things that are well pleasing to thee. For thou,

Christ our God, art the source of light to our souls and bodies, and to thee we ascribe glory, with thine eternal Father and thine all-holy, righteous and life-giving Spirit, now and for ever and from all ages to all ages.

The reading was followed by another series of prayers, for bishops, priests, monks, and for the imperial family; and there was a litany for the departed.

After another litany for peace, the celebrant and the deacon sang the Cherubic Hymn, beginning,

We, who mystically represent the Cherubim, sing the Thrice-holy Hymn to the life-giving Trinity. Let us put away all worldly care, for we are now to receive the King of All, invisibly escorted by the Angelic Hosts . . .

Now the celebrant and the deacon entered the sanctuary, took the paten and the chalice containing the elements from the altar, and went round the nave of the church, preceded by acolytes bearing lighted tapers. They recited prayers as they went. This was the Great Entrance.

Bearing the elements, the ministers entered the sanctuary again and placed the chalice and paten on the altar. Another litany of supplication was recited by the deacon and the choir, and the celebrant said the Offertory Prayer:

O Lord God Almighty, who only art holy, who dost accept the sacrifice of praise from such as call upon thee with their whole heart, accept and receive also unto thy holy altar the prayer of us sinners, enabling us to present unto thee both gifts and spiritual sacrifices for our own sins and for the ignorances of the people: and count us worthy to find such favor before thee, that both our sacrifice may be acceptable unto thee, and the good Spirit of thy grace may rest upon us, and upon these gifts set forth, and upon all thy people.

Ministers and people then joined in reciting the Creed, and the Offertory began. The deacon went into the sanctuary and reverently began to fan the elements, using a metal fan of silver or gold, mounted on a long wooden staff, engraved to represent the six wings of the Seraphim. The celebrant next recited the prayer of thanksgiving and praise which was an eloquent confession of the goodness of God and his benefactions to men. The affirmation that his benefits are both "known and unknown, seen and unseen," shows the working of the Greek mind which acknowledges its limitations, in the presence of the unsearchable nature of God, and realizes that there are things which cannot, in this life, be known or seen:

It is meet and right to praise thee, to glorify thee, to bless thee, to give thanks to thee, to worship thee, in all places of thy dominion, for thou art God ineffable, incomprehensible, invisible, unsearchable, existing always as thou dost exist, thou and thine only-begotten Son and thy Holy Spirit. Thou hast brought us from nothingness into being, and when we fell away didst raise us up again, and thou ceasest not until thou hast done everything, to bring us to Heaven, and to confer on us thy Kingdom to come. For all these things we give thanks to thee and to thine only-begotten Son and to thy Holy Spirit, for all the things we know and do not know, for the seen and unseen benefits which we enjoy. We render thanks to thee also for this service which thou dost deign to receive at our hands, though thou art surrounded by thousands of archangels and ten thousands of angels, by the Cherubim and Seraphim that are six-winged, full of eyes, and soar aloft on their wings . . .

With this, the service began to draw near its climax. The celebrant proceeded to describe the Last Supper, and at the breaking of the bread, he recited the words of Christ, "Take, eat; this is my body which is broken for you, for the remission of sins." When he described how Christ took the cup, the priest again repeated the words, "Drink ye all of this; this is my blood of the new covenant, which is shed for you and for many for the remission of sins." Here the prayer enumerated all the actions of Christ which gave the communion its meaning; for here we are, the priest says,

> commemorating the command of our Savior, and all that was endured for our sake, the Cross, the grave, the Resurrection after three days, the Ascension into Heaven, the enthronement at the right hand of the Father, and the second and glorious coming again—we bring before thee thine own, from thine own, in all things and for all things.

As these words were spoken, the deacon elevated the paten and the chalice, crossing his arms as he did so. At this point the celebrant began the long and beautiful prayer in which he called upon God to send down his Holy Spirit upon the people and their gifts, making the bread the precious Body of Christ, and making the cup his precious Blood, changing them, through the Holy Spirit, so that they might bring to those who receive them the means for the purification of the soul, the remission of sins, the fellowship of the Holy Spirit, and the fulfilment of the Kingdom of Heaven. One of the prayers said at this point gave typical expression to the constant awareness of the unity of all the faithful. The priest prayed that the bread and wine might

> unite us all, as many as are partakers in the one bread and cup, one with another, in the participation of the one Holy Spirit: to suffer no one of us to partake of the holy body and blood of thy Christ unto judgment or unto condemnation; but that thereby we may find mercy and grace together with all the saints which have been well pleasing unto thee since the world began, our forefathers and fathers, patriarchs, prophets, apostles, preachers, evangelists, martyrs, confessors, teachers, and with all the spirits of the just in faith made perfect.

The long prayer continued, commemorating the Virgin Mary; John the Baptist, the Forerunner; the apostles and saints; the faithful departed (mentioning any whose names had been given to the celebrant); all ecclesiastical rulers and Christian ministers; the Emperor and Empress and their court; the army; the city and those who dwelt in it; travellers; the sick; the suffering and captives (in the hands of the barbarians). To the priest's prayer, the deacon added the prayer that the Lord be mindful "of those whom each of us hath in mind, and of all men and women."

Two paragraphs toward the end of this prayer reflect with special clarity the Church's concern for all its members and for every aspect of their lives:

> Remember, O Lord, the people here present, with them that for reasonable cause are absent, and have mercy upon them and us, according to the multitude of thy mercies. Fill their garners with all manner of

good: preserve their marriages in peace and concord: nourish the infants, bring up the youth, succor the aged, comfort the weak-hearted, gather together them that are scattered abroad, bring back them that are strayed and unite them to thy holy catholic and apostolic Church: set free them that are vexed with unclean spirits: sail with the voyagers, fare with the wayfarers, champion the widows, shelter the orphans, deliver the captives, heal the sick. Them that are now under trial, or condemned to the mines or bitter labor in exile, with all in affliction or any necessity and sore beset, remember, O God, with all that have need of thy great tender mercy, both such as love us and such as hate, and them that have charged us to pray for them.

And all thy people remember, O Lord our God, and upon all pour out the wealth of thy mercy, imparting to all their petitions, unto their salvation. And them that we have not remembered, either from ignorance or from forgetfulness or from the number of names, remember thou, O God, which knowest the age and appellation of each, which knowest each from the womb of his mother: for thou, O Lord, art the help of the helpless, the hope of the hopeless, the savior of them that are tempest-tossed, the harbor of voyagers, and the physician of them that are sick: be thou thyself all things to all men, which knowest each and his petition, each house and its need. Keep this city, O Lord, and every city and country from famine, plague, earthquake, flood, fire and sword, from onset of aliens and civil strife.

After prayers of thanksgiving and another litany, the celebrant again invoked the mystical presence of Christ:

... come and sanctify us, thou who sittest above with

the Father and art here invisibly present with us, and do thou deign by thy mighty power to give to us of thy sacred Body and of thy precious Blood.

The celebrant then partook of the elements himself, and administered the communion to the deacon. This was done with the doors of the sanctuary closed. After the ministers had said a prayer of thanksgiving, the doors of the sanctuary were opened and the congregation came forward to receive the communion. Before administering the elements, the priest said a further prayer as a final declaration and petition just before the bread and wine were distributed:

> I believe, Lord, and I acknowledge that thou art of a truth the Christ, the Son of the Living God, which came into the world to save sinners, of whom I am chief. I believe also that this is indeed thy most pure body, and that this is indeed thy precious blood. Therefore, I pray thee, have mercy upon me, forgive me mine offences, voluntary and involuntary, whether in word or deed, whether witting or unwitting: and count me worthy to partake without condemnation of thy most pure mysteries, unto remission of sins and unto everlasting life . . .

Each communicant, as he came forward, bowed and crossed his hands on his chest, while the priest, taking up the bread and wine together in a spoon, placed them in the mouth of the communicant.

When all the congregation had received the communion, the deacon, holding the paten over the chalice, recited the hymns of the Resurrection. These declared the power of Christ, who, slain after the institution of the Last Supper, rose again so that all men might partake of him:

We have seen Christ's resurrection, let us worship the Lord Jesus, for that he is holy, he only is without sin . . . For, behold, from the cross is come joy unto all the world . . . O thou great Passover and hallowed above all, O Christ! O thou the Wisdom [*sophia*] and the Word and Power of God! Grant that we may partake of thee more truly, in that day of thy kingdom which shall have no night.

After a litany of thanksgiving, the priest, while cleansing the sacred vessels, recited a prayer which summarizes the nature of the whole service, in which the faithful have come together to commemorate the sacrifice, death, and resurrection of Christ, and to partake of the joy and power which he brought:

Finished and perfected, so far as is in our power, is all the mystery of thy dispensation, Christ our God. For we have held the remembrance of thy death, we have seen the figure of thy resurrection, we have been filled with thine unending life, we have had fruition of thine inexhaustible delight: wherefor be thou pleased that we all be accounted worthy in the world to come, by the grace of thine unbegotten Father, and thy holy and gracious and life-giving Spirit, now and for ever and world without end.

The priest then blessed the people and went into the sanctuary, closed the doors, and said a final personal prayer of thanksgiving. After the singing of the Song of Symeon ("Lord, now lettest thou thy servant depart in peace . . .") and other hymns and prayers, the priest put off his vestments, and the service was at an end.

The believer, present at the liturgy and receiving the Body and Blood of Christ, was both an individual and a member of a community, the Church. The whole liturgy was a corporate act of the people of God, led by their ministers. It was not the ministers alone who were essential, by their consecration, for the performance of the liturgy. The people too were essential, for the liturgy could not have been complete without them. Indeed, without the people it would have had no meaning.

Both as he heard the service, and as he received the bread and wine, the believer had direct experience of the fellowship of the Church. By receiving the elements, he was marked as an individual servant of God and as a member of the great cloud of witnesses, past, present, and to come. This was a corporate act in which the Church gave perpetual assurance to the faithful of their membership in the community.

Further, the believer was constantly made aware that the liturgy did not embrace only the ordinary members of the Church. He was reminded throughout the service that the liturgy—and the Church as a whole—comprehended the entire state, including the sovereigns, the ecclesiastical and secular rulers, the imperial court, and the army. Detailed prayers for all those in authority, naming specifically the rulers of the empire, were said twice during the liturgy, once just after the reading of the lessons, again in the hymn just before the communion. The sovereigns were described as "lovers of Christ, guarded by God." The priest prayed, "Remember now the most pious and most faithful Emperor whom thou didst judge worthy to rule upon earth . . . Speak in his heart good things concerning thy Church and all thy people." Similar prayers were said a third time in the preliminary service in which the offerings were prepared. A mere duplication, if it were really only duplication, could have been avoided at the beginning, or one superfluous set of prayers could have been eliminated. But this was not mere duplication; the prayers were said twice because there were two occasions on which it was felt they should be said, and it was a sign of their importance that they were repeated. The unity of the Church and the brotherhood of all its members, and the identity of the Church with the government and the nation, were no mere perfunctory ideas.

The same is true of the prayers said in commemoration of the dead. These prayers are elaborate and detailed, and they too appear twice in the Liturgy, once following the reading of the Gospel, again in the prayer for the Church said before communion. A third set of similar prayers occurs in the service for the preparation of the offerings. Once more it is plain that the liturgy intended to stress the bond between the dead and the living, the real existence of the other world and its close connection with this one. These prayers could have been consolidated if it had seemed desirable, but the priests who shaped and used the liturgy considered it more important to commemorate the dead at the points where this remembrance seemed fitting.

The political significance of the liturgy was implicit in the nature of the meeting. When the congregation gathered with its ministers at the liturgy, it was a meeting of people who were at the same time fellow members of the Church and fellow members of the state. By their meeting, they affirmed their solidarity in the Church, and their having met on these terms implied a corresponding solidarity in the state. The liturgy was the possession of the people, not only of a limited number of persons who met on certain occasions in a specific church, but of the people of the nation as a whole. They understood that the liturgy had been the possession of their parents and of their ancestors, and they were confident that it would be handed on, unchanged and undiminished (and this was important), to their children and to the Christians of the future. Living in the present world which was so closely linked with the other world, they would continue to accept the existence, in the one world and the other, of things "known and unknown, seen and unseen." This was the Greek Christian inheritance, the living tradition of a living Church.

When the liturgy carried such implications in the life of the community and of the state, it was not only a national possession, it was a national resource—a source of pride, comfort, faith, hope. If it was an ever-renewed source of spiritual strength for the Greek Christian people, it could not fail to be a source of national pride and national strength for the citizens of the state, who were the same people.

And so the liturgy was in reality one of the most powerful forces in the empire of which Constantinople, with its Church of St. Sophia, was the head. The Emperor, when he attended a celebration of the liturgy, was a very meaningful figure. He came as an individual Christian, as head of the state, and as vicegerent of God on earth and secular head of the Church—and here Justinian took his duties very seriously. When a service such as the Divine Liturgy could be attended by an emperor who was present in such a capacity, people, Church, and state were united in a unique strength—a strength that had its roots in the past, linking the past with the present and preparing the way for the future, all in an unbroken tradition. The Church's liturgy was, like the imperial office, a perpetual institution. If anything, it was more stable. Here was a resource that meant much for the durability of people, state, and civilization. And small wonder was it that the Orthodox Church, as epitomized in the magnificence of St. Sophia as Justinian and later emperors conceived of it, played so vital a role in the religious life of many peoples of central and eastern Europe.

VII

ORTHODOXY AND THE UNITY OF THE STATE

THE CHURCH OF ST. SOPHIA was the magnificent affirmation that the Christian people of the empire, united and orthodox, worshipped under the leadership of the Emperor and the Patriarch. Thus St. Sophia, the "Great Church" of the capital, represented orthodox churches everywhere. As the capital, the city of Constantinople should be the center to which people looked for leadership in their spiritual life. The capital represented the duty of the Emperor, to lead his people to salvation; and to this was joined his duty to save his people from heresy and error which would destroy their souls.

But if the orthodox faith could raise a mighty symbol like St. Sophia, not all the empire followed the orthodoxy of the capital. One of the gravest problems Justinian inherited—perhaps the gravest—was the strength and persistence of the Monophysite heresy in Syria and Egypt. This problem had vexed his predecessors for seventy-five years and it had not been solved. It was not only a major religious issue; it had become a political danger of the first importance. During the whole of Justinian's reign Constantinople was involved in theological debates connected with this problem.

The Monophysite movement had begun after the Fourth General Council of the Church, held at Chalcedon in A.D. 451, though it represented a theological difficulty which was much older. The problem was to understand, and ex-press properly, the relationship between the divine and the human elements in Christ. How were these combined in his person and his actions? Did the two elements remain separate or were they mingled?

The answer to this question was vitally important because it concerned the nature of the redemption of mankind by Christ. Was Christ, in his self-sacrifice and crucifixion, man, or God? Was he, in his humanity, capable of feeling human sufferings, or was he really divine, so that he could not feel and suffer as mortals did? Was his life and experience as God-man real? Was our salvation offered to us by a Christ who was at the same time fully divine and fully human? For some believers, this was the only kind of salvation that could have meaning. This would be a different salvation from one offered by a Christ who was man only in appearance and had no true human experience and sufferings. Some students thought it necessary to stress the reality and completeness of Christ's human nature. While God had come down for man's salvation, it was in a true man that he had manifested himself, and it was because he was completely human that Christ was able to become the Redeemer. But others thought that such a view denied or minimised the divine nature of Christ. Then, if the two elements were united in the one human figure, how were they united? These were questions of the greatest urgency.

At Chalcedon a definition was drawn up which it was hoped would provide for all the points at issue. The formula adopted stated that Christ was perfect in Godhead and perfect in manhood; that he was truly God and truly man; and that he was like us in all things, sin apart. The problem of the relationship of the two elements was met by stating that Christ was "confessed in two natures," divine and human. The natures were not fused, or transmuted one into the other; Christ was not divided into two, and the natures were not dissociated from one another. The properties and operation of the two natures were not changed or diminished. The definition, as it was finally drafted, was put in negative terms.

Theological argumentation had always been a passionate interest of the whole population in the Greek East, where the ancient Greek love of philosophical speculation and disputation had survived in this form. The Greek Church treasured its vigorous tradition of democracy and the laity felt that theological questions concerned them directly. In some quarters, inevitably, discussion was not always well informed, but it was always zealous, and any new theological development immediately became a matter of public concern. In Constantinople, as in every eastern city, one could hear lively theological talk in the streets and shops, as well as at dinner tables. In Byzantium, an absolute monarchy, theology absorbed men's passions in somewhat the same way that politics did in some later societies.

The definition of Chalcedon had represented the effort of the central government to put an end to a vexatious problem. Thus, whatever its theological merits, it had the handicap of being an "official" solution, for it was bound to be treated with suspicion in quarters which were otherwise not in sympathy with the administration. Theologically the formula was unsatisfactory because many people considered that it did not offer a clear and decisive answer to questions about the two natures of Christ. Indeed the very presence in the text of the words "*two* natures" seemed to some thinkers to constitute cause for further debate. The reaction in Syria and Egypt was strong. The oriental minds of the peoples of these regions, retaining some vestiges of old pre-Christian beliefs in savior gods, maintained that Christ the real savior could not be thought of as having humanity like ours, and that the new formula, especially in its treatment of the two natures, was an attack on the true divinity of Christ. Some of the simple folk in these regions felt that an attempt was made to alter their picture of Christ.

Here once more theology became mixed with politics. The people of the empire represented many different nations and traditions—not to mention languages. When these diverse peoples were governed rather autocratically from a capital which represented a different ethnic and linguistic tradition, any matter in which the provinces differed from the central government easily turned into a nationalist cause. The people of Syria and Egypt, many of them illiterate, followed their leaders and believed what they were told.

To the Syrians and the Egyptians the Chalcedonian formula, quite aside from its theological consequences, was something the government in Constantinople was trying to impose on them. Also it was looked upon as a rejection of the theology of the Patriarch Cyril of Alexandria, who was something of a national hero to the Egyptians. So the Monophysite theology developed into a national cause and served to bring into focus all the other grievances of the people against the central government. By the time Justinian became emperor, feeling in Syria and Egypt had risen to an alarming point. How far the authorities in Constantinople understood that local patriotism might turn into separatism, is not clear. What the government did understand, and greatly fear, was that the Monophysites might found a separate church, as the Montanists had done some time before in Asia Minor. This would have brought a real threat to the political cohesion of the empire.

Before Justinian came to the throne, various means of dealing with the Monophysites had been tried, ranging from the conciliation to persecution. The theological problem was formidable, and it may have been, at that time, insoluble; but in this, as in some other matters, the central government in Constantinople treated the provinces in a singularly shortsighted manner. The authorities in the capital, for example, considered it entirely appropriate to choose a Chalcedonian as Patriarch of Alexandria, send him there with an armed guard, and keep him in office by force. In return the Egyptians stayed away from the services in the Patriarch's church. The Monophysite problem was a case in which Constantinople failed to understand or respect the feelings of the people of the provinces. The indigenous races of Syria and Egypt had not absorbed completely the Greek language and the Greek culture, so that when they seemed recalcitrant they were handled by Constantinople as rebellious subjects entitled to no sympathy. Of course the situation had come about partly because the central government had never attempted to assimilate the provincials through education and the spread of the Greek language; indeed free compulsory universal education would have been a strange idea in the world of that time, for the lower classes were thought to be not fit for education. The result was the misunderstanding and violence that accompanied the Monophysite problem.

This was the situation when Justinian became emperor. He was an adherent of the Chalcedonian doctrine, while Theodora, who herself came from the eastern part of the empire, understood and sympathised with the Monophysite point of view. Justinian began by attempting conciliation. He moved as promptly here as he did in his other plans, and in his second year he allowed the heretical bishops and monks, who had been banished for their opinions, to return from exile. Two years later, in 531, he called a conference in Constantinople at which he hoped orthodox and Monophysite leaders would discuss their differences peaceably. Nothing came of the meeting.

Having failed in this, Justinian turned to persecution, and in Syria Monophysites were imprisoned, tortured, and executed. All the while the Monophysite leaders kept in touch with the Empress and she maintained some of them in hiding in the Great Palace itself. People in Constantinople realized that Justinian and Theodora, backing different sides, seemed to be working at cross purposes. The Empress's activities were such common knowledge that the only way people could explain them was by supposing that the Emperor was quite aware of what Theodora was doing, and that the two had decided on this scheme because they thought it would put them in a stronger position in dealing with both sides.

The problem being both religious and political, Justinian became fully involved. Like many of his contemporaries he had always been a keen student of the Scriptures, and he shared the interest of all his people in theology. Seeking to discover what was really at issue in the Monophysite problem, and hoping to be able to find the solution himself, Justinian soon became an expert theologian, and his writings show that he made himself well acquainted with the major theological literature. The Emperor was widely praised in Constantinople for his zeal and learning. There was no lack of priests and monks who were willing to instruct the Emperor, and Procopius—who privately disapproved of Justinian's theological activities—wrote sarcastically in the *Secret History* of the way in which the Emperor might be seen late at night sitting in a corner of the palace discussing theology with a circle of monks.

In his personal study of the Monophysite problem, Justinian went further than any of his imperial predecessors. Of course it would have been valuable for an emperor to have some expert knowledge while the controversy was being carried on by the protagonists; but Justinian went much further and himself took an active part in the formulation of doctrine and the management of the internal affairs of the Church. Here he behaved as none of the previous emperors had done, and his actions were severely censured.

Justinian's conduct shows that he was led beyond normal bounds by his confidence in himself and by his sense of the urgency of the problem. Officially he recognized the difference between the imperial authority and the priesthood. Each comes from the same source—from God—and each adorns the life of man; but the priesthood is concerned with divine matters, the imperial office with human affairs. When Church and state are in harmony, the whole race will prosper; and to this end the Emperor will respect the priesthood. This was Justinian's official pronouncement.

As for doctrine, the consensus had always been that the faith transmitted by the apostles had been guarded by the Church and the bishops, and that if a formulation of doctrine needed to be made, it must come from a general council of bishops which spoke for the Church, under the guidance of the Holy Spirit. Outside the general councils—which by their nature could not be held frequently—the guidance of church affairs in general was thought of as being in the hands of the Patriarchs of the five oldest and most important sees—the "pentarchy"—Rome, Alexandria, Antioch, Constantinople, Jerusalem. The five Patriarchs, representing the bishops under their jurisdiction, could speak with responsibility and authority on matters of definition and interpretation of doctrine. Rome claimed primacy, on the ground of the Pope's being the successor of St. Peter, the Prince of the Apostles, but whether or not this claim was admitted, Constantinople rightfully claimed its own place as the capital. In effect the Patriarch of Constantinople would be the high ecclesiastical dignitary who was closest to the Emperor. In principle Emperor and Patriarch should have functioned harmoniously because both were within the human polity. Their spheres complemented each other, though the sovereign had a distinct standing as the vicegerent of God on earth, chosen by God to rule. It was the traditional and accepted right of the Emperor to summon councils of the Church.

It was Justinian's own concept of his office—of its responsibility and its opportunities—that led him not only to dictate to the authorities of the Church, when he judged this necessary, but to issue edicts in which doctrine was laid down, unilaterally, without the action of a council. In the face of a man like Justinian, it was difficult indeed for an ecclesiastical dignitary to stand on his rights. At a synod held in A.D. 536, the bishops declared that "it is fitting that nothing be done in the most holy Church contrary to the Emperor's will and command." The Emperor Theodosius the Great had issued legislation enforcing orthodoxy, but he had not made pronouncements on matters of dogma.

Life in Constantinople during nearly the whole of Justinian's reign was enlivened by the maneuvers in the theological contest. Both sides employed all the diplomatic subtleties which had become a regular feature of ecclesiastical politics. The Monophysites—thanks apparently to the Empress—were by no means powerless in the capital. On one occasion they even managed to have Anthimus, Bishop of Trebizond, who was secretly a Monophysite, appointed Patriarch of Constantinople. He was exposed by Pope Agapetus, who visited the capital in the following year; but when he was removed from office and sentenced to banishment, Theodora gave him secret refuge in the palace.

While Syria and Egypt were chronically in disturbance, the successive stages of Justinian's efforts in Constantinople all showed the same determination to find a solution, even if a solution had to be imposed. Beginning with an edict issued in the year 533 which was designed to deal with a preliminary question concerning the Trinity, Justinian proceeded with further unilateral pronouncements which were intended to cut through the difficulties. An edict in 543 condemning the followers of the early theologian Origen, some of whose teachings tended toward Monophysitism, was followed in a few years by another directed against some of the theologians who were supposed to have been responsible for the Monophysite position at Chalcedon. This aroused great uneasiness in the West, and the Pope, Vigilius, was brought from Rome to Constantinople so that he might be more easily persuaded to support the Emperor's theology.

The Pope remained in Constantinople for seven years, from 547 until after the Fifth General Council in 553. During part of this time he was virtually a prisoner in the mansion in which he had been lodged. Threats and even force were used on occasion to induce him to accept Justinian's will, and during his whole sojourn Vigilius had to struggle constantly to secure a theology satisfactory in the West, where the controversy was not viewed in the same terms as in the East. The Pope alternately yielded and resisted, but never entirely pleased the Emperor.

Some of the episodes in the contest became famous in the history of Constantinople. At one point, when Pope Vigilius was making a stand against the Emperor, a rumor came to him that he was to be removed from his residence by force. Trusting in the recognized custom by which fugitives could find sanctuary at the altar of a church, the Pope, with his companion the Archbishop of Milan, took refuge in the Church of St. Peter and St. Paul, near the Great Palace. When the Pope's flight became known, a crowd gathered in the church; and when the report was carried to the Emperor, soldiers were sent to remove the two fugitives. When the soldiers arrived, the Pope and the Archbishop, believing that their position would be respected, clung to the altar. The soldiers, however, had orders to remove the Pope, and they seized him by his beard and his feet, and tried to drag him away. The Pope was a powerful man and he was able to keep his hold on the altar. In the struggle, the altar itself gave way and fell over on the Pope. Vigilius was not seriously hurt, but the soldiers were so frightened that they gave up their attempt and left the church.

At length the Fifth General Council, summoned by Justinian to meet in the Secretariat of St. Sophia in 553, confirmed the Emperor's edicts and reaffirmed the Chalcedonian formula, in terms which it was hoped would satisfy the Monophysites. But if Justinian was able to enforce his will in Constantinople, he had no success in Syria and Egypt. Nothing, it seemed, could prevail against the ancient tradition of the Egyptians. The Orientals refused to accept the results of the Fifth General Council. The Emperor continued his efforts, but he was not able to find a basis for peace. Toward the end of his life, as a result of his anxious attempts to discover a solution, he even reached a position in which he appeared to stand with the extreme opponents of Monophysitism, who were themselves heretics.

The term Cæsaropapism, meaning the exercise of supreme authority over ecclesiastical matters by the secular ruler, has become indissolubly linked with the name of Justinian, in the pejorative sense that he sometimes took too much power in religious affairs. In some matters the charge of Cæsaropapism would be unjustified, since Justinian was indeed, by virtue of the source of his imperial office, responsible head of the Church, in administrative procedures, for example. But of course there was very much a question whether he was entitled to assert his authority in matters of doctrine, as he did. But to Justinian, Cæsaropapism, with depreciatory implication, did not exist. In all his high-handed and even violent actions Justinian was guided by his conception of the imperial ideal and by his determination to restore religious unity among his people. He failed because he attempted too much and because the forces against which he was fighting were too strong. Here Constantinople did not see its ruler's dream fulfilled.

VIII

"ATHENS AND JERUSALEM"

OUR VISITOR, standing in the Augustæum, looking up at the statue of Justinian on its column, would notice certain details of the imperial iconography. The Emperor was wearing what was at that time known as the armor of Achilles, that is, half boots (without greaves), a breastplate "in the heroic fashion," and a helmet of the same style. But the Emperor carried no weapon. Instead he held in his left hand the symbol of the power of the Christian Roman Emperor, the globe, which signified his dominion over land and sea, and on the globe was a cross, emblem of the source of his rule and of his victory in war. The statue faced the East and the Emperor's right hand was stretched out, bidding the Persians to remain at home.

Victory in war was one of the official traditional attributes of the Roman Emperor, and Justinian had indeed been able to defeat the Persians. In this respect the statue was eminently appropriate. What might at first seem a little incongruous was the representation of the Emperor in the armor of Achilles. It was true that the ancient Greek hero had been the champion of Hellenism against the barbarians who came from the East; but was it fitting to depict the Christian Emperor in the costume of the pagan warrior? There might even be a faintly comic note here. Justinian was himself a man of distinctly sedentary disposition, and he seems to have been inclined to gain weight easily, but it was not, apparently, considered unsuitable to show him in the armor of the young hero who had not his peer in beauty, swiftness, strength, and valor.

In reality, Justinian as Achilles was a natural example of the fusion of classical culture with Christianity which was one of the great distinguishing marks of education and literature in the age of Justinian. His reign saw a flowering of literature such as the Græco-Roman world had not enjoyed for many years.

This flowering was the end of a long development. The earliest Christians avoided the worldly learning of "the Greeks," with their "philosophy and vain deceit," and saw no way in which their blasphemous literature could be brought into any sort of relationship with Christian life and teaching. As late as the turn of the second and third century, the reaction of many Christians to pagan art and literature was summed up in Tertullian's famous phrase, "What has Athens to do with Jerusalem?" For the pagan, literature and religion (or philosophy) were inseparable, and the early Christians, reared in a pagan world, held the same view. In time, however, Christian thinkers began to realize that there was much in pagan literature that a Christian might read with profit. Plato, for example, sometimes seemed to approximate Christian thought. After Christianity had been emancipated, thoughtful Christian teachers such as St. Basil the Great, who had had a careful training in Greek literature, were able to show that pagan literature need not be wholly abandoned, and that much good could come from study of the best parts of it. St. Basil and his colleagues did not feel that their faith would be threatened by some aspects of Greek literature which earlier generations of Christians had found repugnant, and obviously dangerous for the nurture of Christian children. It was true that such literary themes as the loves of the Olympian gods, and the robust humor of Aristophanes, represented a view of life that Christianity had come to replace. But St. Basil and other thinkers had the insight to perceive that it was possible to make a basic distinction, and to separate good and bad elements in classical literature. The existence of undesirable motifs—which could after all be ignored—need not mean that no use could be made of the rest.

Here was established a conviction which was vital for the future of Christian culture. It meant, in fact, the possibility of the development of a *new* Christian culture, subsuming and utilizing the best of ancient thought, which was to have enormous importance for the future of civilization. Such a process was not to be completed quickly, and indeed the final step remained for Justinian, who perceived that even in his day the end had not been reached, and that something still needed to be done to bring the new culture to its ultimate development.

In terms of education, the realization that classical culture need not be wholly abandoned meant that the characteristic elements of pagan literature which had dominated education since the great days of Athens—the ethical teaching, the philosophical training, the schooling in clarity and good taste in expression—all could be utilized in the intellectual training of Christians, within the framework of Christian thought and belief. St. Basil, in his celebrated letter to his nephews on the value of the classics, had made it plain that scholars and teachers could both properly and profitably employ the best works of the ancient writers in education and in the production of Christian literature.

The acceptance of this view solved a fundamental problem of pedagogy. The social and intellectual system of the world into which Christianity came had been based on the view that the classical writers—poets, historians, orators, philosophers—had set down the best account of humanity in all its aspects that one could find. The proper study of mankind was man, and it was through careful examination of these classic pictures of human nature and conduct, as it had been recorded by the greatest writers of antiquity, that a young man would best be prepared for life, both public and private. Moreover, training in the literary style and the eloquence of the ancient writers was the best preparation of the mind, for clear speech and writing represented clear thought. The great models of antiquity had never been surpassed; hence the best education was the study and imitation of the ancient masters. This educational program was not intended to be slavish copying (though it could at its worst degenerate into that). It simply represented the view that since everyone agreed that it was impossible for later generations to improve on the classical masters, it was to them that the student and the teacher must turn.

Even after Christianity had grown to the point where numbers of prominent men were Christians, public life was still in the hands of men who had had this type of education. By this time, too, the educational system had come to be looked upon as the embodiment of the whole ancient heritage, political and philosophical as well as literary. In the Greek East, even in the days of subjugation to Rome, Greek literature kept alive the tradition of the political, intellectual, and artistic achievement of the greatest Greek writers of the fifth and fourth centuries B.C. To give up this educational and literary tradition because some parts of classical literature were indelicate would have been to lose a great deal. It would have meant, indeed, that a Greek Christian, deprived of his literary heritage, and trained solely in Christian writings, would be cut off from a major part of his national inheritance.

It was into an intellectual world founded on this base that Justinian came. If many centuries ago Greek culture had captured its captor Rome, it had continued to exert its authority over minds from non-Greek lands which came under its influence. The young man's mind—and his career showed that it was an exceptional mind—responded to classical civilization as he found it in Constantinople, and like many another newcomer Justinian recognized the meaning of the classic spirit and set himself to absorb it, and be absorbed by it. The Greek language itself fascinated him and he took pleasure in composing state papers, though there was a skilled secretariat at his disposal for that purpose. One can imagine that the members of the secretariat read their imperial master's compositions with a critical eye. Procopius in his *Secret History* tells us rather wickedly that the Emperor also took great pleasure in performing the public reading of his documents himself in spite of the provincial accent which he never lost when speaking Greek. (But who was to convey it to the Emperor that his accent was provincial?)

As Justinian studied the needs of the state, and in particular as he considered plans to make a final end to paganism and heresy, he saw that there was one problem which was fundamental not only for education but for the fulfillment of Greek Christian culture. This problem was the teaching of pagan literature and philosophy in the schools and universities.

Whether or not he saw it in just these terms, the situation that faced Justinian was, in its political and cultural implications, the same problem that the Emperor Julian the Philosopher (A.D. 361–363) had found. Of course the pagan Julian and the Christian Justinian were working in exactly opposite directions. Julian, attempting to revive paganism and eliminate Christianity, had forbidden Christians to teach classical literature in the schools, since it was dishonest for a man to teach something he did not believe in; such a teacher obviously might corrupt his pupils. What Justinian found was that classical literature and philosophy were being taught in two ways. In Constantinople, and in Gaza and Alexandria, the chief centers of advanced education at that time, the classics were taught by professors who were themselves Christians, and wrote both theological treatises and literary works in the classical style. It was at Gaza that men such as the historian Procopius were trained, under a succession of famous teachers of literature whose careers and writings can be traced in detail beginning with the reign of the Emperor Anastasius. Procopius of Gaza (not related to the historian Procopius of Cæsarea) was typical of these Christian professors. He wrote an enormous commentary on the Octateuch and a commentary on Isaiah as well as some polemical treatises. At the same time he composed a panegyric of the Emperor Anastasius in the classical manner, a lament on an earthquake at Antioch, a description of a mechanical clock at Gaza, and an elaborate description in rhythmic prose of two pictures at Gaza showing scenes of the story of Phædra and Hippolytus. Procopius' pupil and successor Choricius wrote panegyrics of his former fellow student Marcianus, who had become a bishop, which included detailed descriptions of two churches at Gaza. He also composed pieces in the classical style, fictitious speeches by historical personages, nuptial songs, and other poetry. These classical forms were cultivated for their value in rhetorical training; and the Christian professors, well known as authors of ecclesiastical works, would appear in the theatres of Gaza to give public exhibitions in which they declaimed before enthusiastic audiences their rhetorical compositions. At Alexandria, a famous center of scientific and philosophical studies since the Hellenistic period, the work was similar. In Justinian's day one of the most celebrated scholars there was John, surnamed Philoponus ("Lover of Work"), who wrote both theological treatises and polemics, and commentaries on Aristotle. The teaching of these centers was acceptable since these Christian professors presented classical literature to their students from the Christian point of view.

But there was one center which had never associated itself with the Christian program of classical studies. This was Athens, still a university town, though much reduced in its activities and its influence, and no longer producing distinguished pupils. At Athens the professors were still pagans, and in their little circle they continued to teach classical Greek philosophy in the old manner. Instruction of this kind was obviously an anachronism, and teachers who carried on such a program were not to be trusted. It was not the teaching of classical philosophy that was dangerous—one could study the philosophers at Gaza and Alexandria, as well as at Constantinople. What was wrong was the teaching of classical philosophy by men who did not believe in Christianity. Justinian gave the professors at Athens an opportunity to become Christians, but they declined to take this way of saving their jobs, and Justinian had no choice but to close the schools. This was in A.D. 529, Justinian's second year as emperor. The Athenian professors went as refugees to the court of the King of Persia (where in time they found themselves so unhappy that they petitioned to be allowed to return home). Athens had outlived its role; its old function had passed to the new Christian schools. Of course closing the pagan schools did not put an immediate end to paganism in the empire; but Justinian's action, taken so promptly after he became sole ruler, served as a definitive declaration of what Christian education, based on the classics, was to be in the future. The culture of Constantinople had supplanted that of Athens.

Indeed the favorable atmosphere of the capital produced a number of distinguished literary figures, most of them connected with the government or the court. One of the characteristic careers was that of John the Lydian, lawyer, scholar, and civil servant, who tells us in some autobiographical passages about the scholarly side of government service. When he came to Constantinople as a young man, looking for a post, it was some time before he was able to find a position. While waiting, he tells us, he spent his time studying Aristotle and Plato. Then, when he had been given a post in the legal section of the office of the prætorian prefect, he wrote a short poetic encomium on the head of his office, who had made it possible for him to have his position. His chief rewarded him with a gold piece for every verse of the panegyric. The encomium was doubtless worth something to the recipient. John was appointed to the office of the legal counsel, where all the officials, he says, were distinguished by an excellent education and took pains over their Latin, which was essential for legal work, and was a strange language to most of them, including John. As he advanced in his career, John was able to devote an increasing amount of time to study, and in due course he married his chief's daughter. He speaks of his uncle, an official in the same department, as "a wise man and a lover of learning." In time John's passion for scholarship came to the notice of the Emperor himself, and John's career was made. Justinian first invited him to compose an encomium on himself, and John had the honor of delivering this before the Emperor in the presence of some distinguished visitors from Rome who happened to be in Constantinople at the time. The panegyric was so successful that the Emperor commanded John to write a history of the Persian War.

Justinian also intervened personally to advance John's career. He issued an order to John's superior which shows the real esteem in which literary excellence was held in the civil service. John quotes the order (it is interesting to note that it was very likely composed by the Emperor himself):

> In the most learned John, We have perceived knowledge of literature, skill in language and grace in poetry, in addition to his wide learning; and We have seen that he has made himself, by his own labors, most accomplished in the Latin tongue, and that while he has borne himself nobly in the service of Your Excellency's legal staff, he has also chosen, in addition to that service, to devote his life to study, and to dedicate himself wholly to literature. Believing that it would be unworthy of Our times to leave without reward a man who has attained such a degree of merit, We command Your Excellency to reward him from the public treasury with such and such payment [John when he quotes the document tactfully suppresses the figure]. Also let this most learned man know that We do not stop with this, but that We shall honor him with greater appointments and Imperial generosities, thinking it unseemly that such eloquence should receive small reward, and praising him if he will share with many others the talent he possesses.

The Emperor ordered that John be appointed professor of law in the Imperial Law School in Constantinople, in addition to his other duties. This post, John notes with satisfaction, gave him great prestige.

And so, after forty years and four months of service, John came to the age of retirement. He had made a considerable private fortune. A ceremony was held to mark his retirement, and his superior read a citation, in the presence of all his colleagues, in which he praised John's faithful performance of his duties and his services to literature and learning. John was now able to devote himself wholly to his books, and the remainder of his life was devoted to study and writing.

John the Lydian's career, while distinguished, was by no means unique. Indeed it was natural, in the Constantinople of those times, for an educated gentleman to have a taste for literary composition. If he wrote correct verse in the classical manner, this was a sign that he possessed the best education and culture, and the leisure to make use of his elegant accomplishment. Men in public life were frequently scholars and poets. The *Greek Anthology*, for example, preserves selected specimens of the verses of nine such poets of the time of Justinian who were lawyers, jurists, civil servants, or members of the imperial household.

Two such men of letters were the leading literary figures of Constantinople in Justinian's reign—Procopius of Cæsarea, the historian, a judge advocate in the army, and Paul the Silentiary, a functionary in the Great Palace. Both served Justinian well with their writings.

Procopius, a historian of real gifts, had his education in his native city in Palestine and in Gaza, then a delightful small university town. The young men who went there to perfect their literary studies were trained to admire and imitate the greatest of the classical historians, Herodotus and Thucydides. Procopius obviously had a talent, and he made himself thoroughly familiar with their styles and methods.

When his training in literature had been completed, Procopius turned to study of the law—for here the ability to speak and write with both eloquence and elegance was indispensable for a successful career, and judges and clients were impressed by an advocate who showed that he had made himself familiar with the greatest minds of antiquity. A young man with both legal training and literary flair was sure of advancement.

We find Procopius in Constantinople in the year 527—the year Justinian became sole emperor—as a legal adviser on the staff of Belisarius, at the time when the brilliant young general was being sent to Syria to deal with the Persian inroads. Assigned to Belisarius' staff while still a young man himself, Procopius found that he was in an ideal situation for a man who wished to pursue a literary career. It was in fact an opportunity, which Procopius fully exploited, to become the leading historian of the day. While he may not have realized it when he joined Belisarius' staff, Procopius was to be attached for fifteen years or more, in an important and confidential capacity, to a man who was to become the most brilliant of Justinian's generals, and one of the greatest military figures of all time. Procopius soon became an enthusiastic admirer of Belisarius, and he made use of his opportunities as companion and adviser to the general to begin work on a history of Justinian's wars which made a great success as it was published in parts during the reign.

Procopius was conscious that the period of which he was writing was a great one, and that he was describing the accomplishments of a great emperor who was restoring the empire to its ancient glory. Procopius, like his contemporaries, saw Justinian as a remarkable man—however much one might dislike him or fear his policies. In the history of the empire, this promised to be a memorable reign, and Procopius hoped that it was from his work that future generations would learn about it.

And it is characteristic of the era that Procopius chose, for his literary form, the style of Thucydides, with touches from Herodotus. His audience must have expected something like this, and Procopius' skill as an imitator of the ancient historians was an important factor in the success of his work. The present might bring new enemies to the empire, new problems and dangers, even the new ideas and bold policies of Justinian, but it was still Thucydides who had set the highest standards of historical writing. Justinian's reign might be a new epoch in history, but it was still to be viewed as a part of the great past, and depicted in the literary form which had made that past familiar.

The first part of Procopius' history was written between the years 545 and 550, when Justinian's program no longer enjoyed the success of its earlier years. When the work began to be published in parts—probably read aloud by the author at gatherings of distinguished guests—it must have come to the Emperor's notice immediately. In the midst of his disappointments, Justinian must have been pleased with this splendid record of his earlier years. One result was that about 559 or 560 the Emperor commanded Procopius to compose an account of his building activities. Procopius' monograph was a carefully wrought panegyric in which Justinian's vast construction program was described with all the resources of literary art. The Emperor did not realize that all the while this distinguished author was writing a scandalous *Secret History*, not to be published until after his death, in which he cruelly libelled the Emperor and Empress who, he believed, had failed to do justice to his hero Belisarius. The secret volume was kept well hidden, and Procopius ended his career in positions of dignity and respect.

Such was the life work of the foremost historian of Justinian's day. We know less of the training and career of the leading poet, Paul the Silentiary. His title is that of an usher—*silentiarius*—who guarded the doors when the Imperial Council was in session, or when the Emperor was granting an audience. This was a ceremonial post, assigned to a gentleman; the silentiaries were respected members of the Court, though not of the highest rank.

As Procopius was a follower of Herodotus and Thucydides, Paul went back to Homer. His famous description of Justinian's new Church of St. Sophia was written in 887 hexameters—about the length of one of the longer books of Homer—with an introduction in the iambic verse which had become popular for rhetorical purposes. While Paul names Homer as his model, he also imitates the more recent epic poet Nonnus, who had undertaken to translate Homer's simpler style into a more sophisticated form. How old Paul may have been when this work was written, in 562, we do not know; but behind this brilliant and assured performance there must have been much practice and training.

Homer becomes the vehicle for the praise of the noblest church in the empire. Like Procopius' much briefer prose panegyric of the church, a part of his monograph on the Emperor's buildings written a few years earlier, Paul's account of the spiritual effect of the building on the worshipper reflects real Christian feeling. Throughout the poem, of course, there runs the theme of the greatness of Justinian as a builder. As Procopius' works had come opportunely, when the Emperor was beginning to be disappointed in his undertakings, Paul's poem in praise of the Emperor and his great church was timely. In September, 560 a false rumor of Justinian's death caused riots, and in the year 562 a plot against his life was discovered. It is likely that it was in this year that Paul was selected for his known skill as a poet and commanded to write his panegyric for the dedication in December, 562 of the rebuilt dome of the church.

But Paul the Silentiary was not famous for his description of St. Sophia alone. He was, in his own day and later, one of the most appreciated Byzantine writers of occasional verses in the classical manner, and the contrast between these and his Christian description of the Church of St. Sophia illustrates vividly the dualism in the literary world of Justinian's age. The seventy-eight of Paul's epigrams which are preserved in the *Greek Anthology* show that he was an accomplished practitioner of the classical style, with an intimate knowledge of pagan literature and a delicate feeling for language and metre.

Some of these epigrams give us delightful glimpses of the literary circles in the official world. We find Paul exchanging epistles in verse with his friend Agathias the lawyer, who was also a historian and poet. Agathias had gone to a villa across the Bosporus from Constantinople to find quiet for his legal studies. He writes to Paul describing the beauty of the countryside. But in spite of all the delights he enjoys in his seclusion he longs for the fair object of his love; and he longs too to see his friend Paul. Paul replies in the same style, giving Agathias advice in the conduct of his career as lover.

Paul has many charming verses on the joys and sorrows of the lover—the perils of clandestine love, the cold mistress, all the themes of the traditional repertory. He tells how Love, like a mad dog, has bitten him, and has turned his soul to frenzy. Or he describes a lovers' quarrel, or tells of a lover waiting for his mistress, who swore she would come, but has not. There are other traditional themes. A hunter dedicates his bow to Apollo. The beauties of Constantinople are described. There is a specimen of the traditional epitaph which speaks to the person who stops to read it.

Agathias' epigrams—one hundred are preserved in the *Greek Anthology*—show a notable talent. He writes, like Paul, of love, ingeniously, lightly, treating a variety of themes from the classical repertory. He describes the lover's sleepless night of anxiety; writes of a bride waiting for her bridegroom; chides his mistress because she is not as sick with love for him as he is for her—but if she is haughty, she will be punished. On other occasions Agathias produced metrical epitaphs in the ancient manner, such as could never have been inscribed on tombstones in Christian Byzantium. And there are dedicatory verses such as the pagan Greeks had written to accompany votive offerings to their gods. A plowman dedicates his land to Pan. There are also many descriptions of pictures. He writes charmingly on the death of a tame partridge which had been killed by a cat. But along with all these academic exercises Agathias wrote Christian epigrams of real feeling, embodying his prayers and those of his friends. Some of these epigrams were inspired by pictures, such as an image of the Archangel Michael which Agathias had seen while traveling. "The eyes," he writes, "stir up the depths of the spirit, and Art can convey by colors the prayers of the soul."

CONSTANTINOPLE

Other epigrams in the *Greek Anthology* are the work of well known government officials. Macedonius left some particularly delicate verses—a lover's apostrophe to the morning star, a lament to an inconstant mistress, the complaint of a wounded lover begging his mistress to allay his longing as she kindled it, a reminder to his mistress that she must not delay, for old age will bring her wrinkles. He also wrote a prayer to Poseidon of an old fisherman about to give up his trade; and he composed graceful thoughts on Pandora's box. Julianus Ægyptius, former governor of a district in Egypt, composed an epitaph of the well-known type in which the dead man exhorts the passer-by to drink, before he puts on the garment of dust. A lawyer named Arabius is remembered as author of an epigram on Pan piping. Leontius, a member of the board of eighteen referees who received petitions addressed to the Emperor and handed down his decisions, left a charming epigram on the death of music—with Orpheus gone and Plato dead, nothing is left.

But we are not to think of Paul, the dignified silentiary and his lawyer friends as dashing lovers, writing stylish verses on their private adventures, or as neo-pagans, worshippers of Pan and Poseidon in secret. The Emperor Justinian was a serious man, and (at least if he knew what they were doing) he would not have had languishing poets about his court. These writers produced their epigrams as literary exercises, to exhibit their skill and taste, and the composition of what really amounted only to academic verse was not to be taken as casting any doubt on their religious status. Greek classical literature was a part of the ancient heritage, and Christianity, as custodian of this heritage, was well able to absorb the classical literary tradition so long as it was understood that the tradition now played the role of an element in the larger Christian culture.

Against such a background we can understand the promptness with which Justinian acted to do away with the pagan teaching at Athens. This might have seemed a very minor episode in the history of the empire, but it had real importance. It was not merely a cultural or a religious question—though both factors were of course involved. This was a case in which literature and philosophy, as the basis of education, affected public life and the health of the state. The study of classical literature, in Justinian's view, was not simply the cultivation of belles-lettres. It was part of the national heritage, and it formed the material for the training of members of the state. True patriotism and national pride would come from the record of the achievements of ancient Greece; and it was Justinian's responsibility to see that the essential base of such a pedagogical system was maintained. Classical literature had been proven over the centuries to be the best educational material, but in the Christian Roman Empire which Justinian hoped to shape, the only teachers who could function properly were Christians.

This was the Christian world's answer—under the ægis of Justinian—to the question of Tertullian. The Greek Christian world had discovered what Tertullian was too passionate to conceive—that there might be a new Athens as well as a new Jerusalem. The new Athens could be both Athenian and Christian; and it was in Constantinople that this was to be found. The classical literature had given an expression of human nature and human intellectual achievement which continued to draw men to it; many of Plato's doctrines bore some resemblance to Christian teachings.

CONSTANTINOPLE

The Greek-speaking citizens of the empire in Justinian's age were very conscious of their descent from the Greeks of ancient times who had produced Homer and Plato, Herodotus and Thucydides, and they saw no essential discontinuity between themselves and classical Greece. Christianity had been added, and now took first place; but the classical heritage continued. Indeed, to destroy or abandon it would have been to do away with one of the essential roots of civilization. Christianity had superseded this root and stood in first place in human life; but since it was supreme, it could afford to allow the classical tradition to remain. The very fact that it remained showed that Christianity had conquered it.

THE GOD-GUARDED CITY

WHAT DID the citizens of Constantinople in the age of Justinian expect of the future?

Their conception of the future was based on two sets of beliefs, one representing the experience of their past history, the other based on Christian teaching. It had been an axiom that the Roman Empire was eternal. And this eternal state was now bound to a church which likewise existed in terms of eternity. It was inconceivable that either should ever be overthrown, or replaced by anything else. There was indeed no other civilization, no other religion, by which they could be replaced. The empire and Christianity were both universal in their claims to represent the true polity and the true religion, and in this sense both could be expected to endure to the end of the world, or the consummation of the ages.

The pride and delight of the East Romans in their past history was very real. They and their ancestors had held off the barbarians and had kept civilization alive. They were sure they possessed a great deal the barbarians did not have. Here the age of Justinian exhibited a correlation that ran all through Byzantine history; for it was when the empire felt itself strongest that it was also most conscious of its close connection with its roots in Greek culture and ancient history. Yet the empire did not think of itself as repeating its past; Procopius for example wrote proudly of the improvements and progress the reign of Justinian had brought.

It was these ideas of the past and the future that helped to shape Justinian's conception of the imperial office and guide his program. If the Emperor was a central figure in Constantinople, he was central in terms of Church, state and people. Justinian was the emperor who had brought this image of the ruler to its fullest embodiment, and in his purposeful reign he asserted the sovereign's role with overwhelming authority. The development of the state had of course been working in this direction, but it was Justinian—more energetic and ambitious and daring than some of his predecessors—who took the final step and created a picture of the ruler and his people which was to be the pattern for the future. It was true that Justinian's program was not altogether successful, but the image had been created, and remained.

Here Constantinople played its role as the physical setting about which the future state was to be centered. Wealthy, cosmopolitan, proud of its position, and in touch with the whole world, the city had by the time of Justinian come to be the true nucleus of the Christian Roman Empire, and this it was to remain until it fell to the Turks in 1453.

What, then, were the sources of the strength with which the Empire of Constantinople maintained itself for so long a time in the face of growing pressures and dangers?

These sources were all to be seen in the age of Justinian. Strength lay, for one thing, in the East Romans' consciousness of the presentness of the past whose achievements gave pride, confidence, and inspiration for the present and prepared a foundation for the future. This sense of the continuation into the present of the ancient tradition of civilization was clearly felt in every department of life—religious, political, intellectual. In the case of the Church, there was both the strong awareness of the historic character of the Body of Christ on earth and the constant understanding—exemplified in the Divine Liturgy—of the bond between members of the Church in this world and those in the next world. From this came the ever-present sense of the reality of the communion of saints and the cloud of witnesses. This was a source of national strength which matched that other source of power and national consciousness in the political past of the state.

From the same elements, strength came from the awareness of the balance and mutual support which existed among the three spheres of life and society—Church, Emperor, and people. In principle, the harmonious association of these three forces was one of the marks, and one of the essential conditions, of civilization. People, conscious that they could depend on this co-operation, could know that their civilization contained its own special element of strength, and that their place in the world was assured.

Continuing strength, too, came from the remarkable ability of this civilization to assimilate newcomers and absorb them into the tradition. The tradition of culture and religion that had this power within itself was bound to have a long life. Also it was bound to give the greatest care to the preservation of the forms in which this tradition was expressed—literature, art, architecture, law.

In Constantinople, the enduring symbol was the equestrian statue of Justinian which stood for the empire defending civilization against the barbarians and keeping alive the Greek tradition in the Christian world. The statue, symbolically, survived until the sixteenth century, when a French visitor to the city, Pierre Gilles, watched it being melted to make cannon. The armor of Achilles and the globe surmounted by the cross suggested another aspect of the sources of strength of the Byzantine state, the unity of faith and culture.

In the Greek Christian world there was no artificial separation between religion and everyday life. All life was lived within the framework of the Church and its teaching. The new culture of Constantinople was a universal culture, like the pagan culture it had replaced, and it was to make a true center for this that the city had been founded. This unity of faith and culture implied a certain belief in the government of the universe and the direction of human life. This belief was taken for granted, and it gave a motivation to all aspects of life that nothing else could. It was the pattern of civilization.

In the city-civilization of Constantinople, man living in a community (in Aristotle's classic statement) reached his highest development. Aristotle had written of the Greek city-state, but in the culture of Justinian's day the relationship of the city and its inhabitants remained much the same. It was still in a city that the individual could best realize his place in the Græco-Roman-Christian culture.

Constantinople the city existed both by itself, as the capital, and in relation to other cities. As the only great city of the Græco-Roman world founded after the triumph of Christianity, it occupied a special place in the succession of eminent cities. Athens and Rome, the other capitals, had grown from remote and even obscure origins, while Alexandria and Antioch had been special foundations of the Hellenistic era, designed and built for a specific purpose in the propagation of Greek culture and political influence in non-Greek territory. Politically, Constantinople had supplanted Athens and Rome, and had taken the leadership over Alexandria and Antioch. But while Constantinople in Justinian's day was the leader among the Græco-Roman cities, it still perforce existed in relation to them. Each of the older cities had transmitted something to Constantinople—something of its own literature, learning, philosophy, theology, architecture or art. Constantinople collected the contributions of its sister cities and shaped them into a new civilization, in which the past lived on, in a new form. But if the lending process was more or less complete in the case of the cities of Athens and Rome themselves, it was still active in the case of the other cities. Antioch, Alexandria, Gaza—particularly the last two—were still making their contributions to the culture of the day, and were still able to produce something that Constantinople could absorb.

This was not, however, the extent of the relationship. If Constantinople was enriched by the life of the other cities, its return to them was not always comparable. In a civilization based on the city, rivalries were between cities, rather than between countries, as they were at a later day. The ancient jealousy between Antioch and Alexandria, for example, was continued in the even greater rivalry between Constantinople and Antioch and between Constantinople and Alexandria. The elements in these jealousies were many—political, theological, linguistic, racial. And to these very old political elements was added the jealousy of the new city, Constantinople, as the capital; for as the capital it was a source of oppression.

Here, it would seem, is one department in which the city-civilization failed in its role of the custodian of culture. Yet in those times this would not necessarily have been thought of as a failure. Each city had its own life and its own tradition. Interference with this tradition, from any outside source, meant loss of local virtue. In the case of a city such as Alexandria, there was the exceptionally strong force of local patriotism, exemplified in the difference of tongues. The natives who still spoke Egyptian, with little or no Greek, could only look upon the Greek culture which came to them from outside as something alien. No one in authority would have thought of trying to teach Greek, and bring Greek culture and Roman historical traditions, to the multitudinous Syrians and Egyptians. Many of them were illiterate anyway. To this extent the exclusive character of the civilization of Constantinople could not be carried far beyond the city itself.

The breach between Constantinople and the subjects in Syria and Egypt showed its effects when the Arabs invaded these countries, in the century following Justinian's, and were welcomed as masters who, it was hoped, would be better than the hated rulers in Constantinople.

This, then, was a failure of the system which produced the city-civilization, even though the failure might not have been understood at the time. But against it must be set the distinguished history of the city during the remaining nine centuries of its existence. The city of Constantine played its true role as the medium by which the continuity from antiquity through the Middle Ages was assured; and as a center of civilization it built up within itself the power to survive the forces of barbarism. The mission of the city was shown by the vitality with which it preserved its significance for civilization even when the territory of the empire was gradually being overrun by the Turks, until for a time almost nothing survived but the city itself. During all this time Constantinople stood for the highest degree of civilization in the world. Indeed, in the world which knew the Dark Ages, no city could match it.

It was thus that Constantinople transmitted the civilization of the Greek-speaking world, pagan and Christian, from antiquity to the Renaissance in western Europe. This was possible only because of the intense loyalty of the Byzantine people to their tradition. The loyalty might be felt, and realized, in different degrees; but it was a common bond and it had a center in a city. The population of Constantinople was a society, of all levels, which, though on occasion somewhat overfond of secular distractions and worldly pleasures, was very conscious of living in a state that was directed by God and guarded by God. The task of the city was something that was always before its people; and such a task was for them a true source of pride.

SELECTED BIBLIOGRAPHY

CONTEMPORARY SOURCES IN TRANSLATION:

Procopius, with an English translation by Henry B. Dewing. 7 vols. London and Cambridge, Mass., Loeb Classical Library, 1914–1961, including the *History of the Wars* (vols. 1–5), the *Secret History* (vol. 6) and the *Buildings of Justinian* (vol. 7, reprinted with additions and corrections, 1961).

The Greek Anthology, with an English translation by W. R. Paton. 5 vols., London and Cambridge, Mass., Loeb Classical Library, 1916–1918, including epigrams and occasional verses of the poets of the age of Justinian. A convenient selection (text and translation), with valuable introduction and notes, is *Select Epigrams from the Greek Anthology*, edited by J. W. Mackail, new edition, London and New York, 1906.

Paul the Silentiary, *Description of the Church of St. Sophia*. Extensive excerpts, in translation or paraphrase, are given in W. R. Lethaby and H. Swainson, *The Church of Sancta Sophia*, London, 1894.

Barker, Ernest (editor), *Social and Political Thought in Byzantium, from Justinian I to the last Palæologus*, Oxford, 1957. Excerpts from literary texts, in translation, with introduction and notes.

The Orthodox Liturgy, being the Divine Liturgy of St.

SELECTED BIBLIOGRAPHY

John Chrysostom and St. Basil the Great. London, Published by the Society for Promoting Christian Knowledge for the Fellowship of Saints Alban and Sergius, 1939 (reprinted 1954). Translation, with introduction, explanatory notes and glossary, of the modern liturgy, which in essentials represents the Byzantine usage.

Justinian, *Digest*, translated by C. H. Monro, 2 vols. Cambridge, Eng., 1904–1909.

———, *Institutes*, translations by T. C. Sandars, London, 1853; J. T. Abdy and B. Walker, Cambridge, Eng., 1876; and J. B. Moyle, 2 vols. Oxford, 1883 (and reprinted).

CONSTANTINOPLE:

Mamboury, E. *Istanbul touristique, édition française*. Istanbul, 1951. Guide book written by an archæologist long familiar with the antiquities of the city.

Les Guides bleus, Turquie. Paris, 1958. A general guide book with a good account of Istanbul.

Grosvenor, E. A. *Constantinople*. 2 vols. Boston, 1895. A comprehensive account of Constantinople ancient and modern, based on intimate knowledge of the city.

Janin, R. *Constantinople byzantine*. Paris, 1950. A detailed account of the city and its monuments in the Byzantine period.

———. *Les églises et les monastères*, in: *La Géographie ecclésiastique de L'Empire byzantin*, Pt. 1, *Le Siège de Constantinople et le patriarcat œcuménique*. Paris. 1953. A comprehensive study of the churches and monasteries.

Swift, E. H. *Hagia Sophia*. New York, 1940. A general account of the building and its history.

Van Nice, R. L. *Saint Sophia in Istanbul: An Architectural Survey*. Washington, D. C., Dumbarton Oaks Center for

Byzantine Studies of Harvard University, 1965. The most complete and accurate survey of the building.

HISTORY OF JUSTINIAN'S REIGN:

Vasiliev, A. A. *Justin the First; An Introduction to the Epoch of Justinian the Great.* Cambridge, Mass., 1950.

Barker, John W. *Justinian and the Later Roman Empire.* Madison, Wis., 1966.

Rubin, Berthold. *Das Zeitalter Iustinians.* Vol. I. Berlin, 1960. The first volume of an exhaustive study.

Stein, Ernest. *Histoire du Bas-Empire*, II: *De la disparition de l'Empire d'Occident à la mort de Justinien (476–565).* Paris and Brussels, 1949.

Jones, A. H. M. *The Later Roman Empire, 284–602: A Social, Economic and Administrative Survey.* Oxford, 1964 (3 vols. and vol. of maps) and Norman, 1964 (2 vols.). An authoritative and comprehensive study, written from the sources.

Bury, J. B. *History of the Later Roman Empire from the death of Theodosius I to the Death of Justinian (A.D. 395–565).* 2 vols. London, 1923, reprinted, New York, 1958. Bury's account of Justinian's reign is in some details out of date, but in other respects is still worth reading.

POLITICAL THEORY:

Dvornik, Francis. *Early Christian and Byzantine Political Philosophy: Origins and Background.* 2 vols. Washington, D.C., Dumbarton Oaks Center for Byzantine Studies of Harvard University, 1966. A detailed and authoritative account, written from the sources.

SELECTED BIBLIOGRAPHY

Henry, Patrick, III. "A Mirror for Justinian: the *Ekthesis* of Agapetus Diaconus," *Greek, Roman and Byzantine Studies*, 8 (1967), 281–308.

Works on Byzantine History and Civilization:

Baynes, N. H., and H. St. L. B. Moss (editors). *Byzantium, An Introduction to East Roman Civilization.* Oxford, 1948 (and reprinted). The best general introductory account in English, containing essays written by various scholars. Includes a valuable bibliography and excellent plates and maps.

Hussey, J. M. *The Byzantine World.* Third edition, revised. London, 1967. The best concise introductory account.

The Cambridge Medieval History. Vol. IV, second edition, in two parts. Cambridge, Eng., 1966–1967. Chapters by various scholars, including studies of aspects of the reign of Justinian.

Baynes, N. H. *Byzantine Studies and Other Essays.* London, 1955. Lucid and penetrating essays by a great Byzantinist, of fundamental importance for any study of Byzantine history and civilization.

Ostrogorsky, Georg. *History of the Byzantine State*, translated by Joan Hussey. Second, revised English edition, translated from the third German edition (1963), Oxford, 1968. The best general political, social and economic history.

Vasiliev, A. A. *History of the Byzantine Empire, 324–1453.* Madison, Wis., 1952 (reprinted in two volumes). A general history, including literature, learning and art.

Diehl, Charles. *Byzantium: Greatness and Decline*, translated by Naomi Walford. New Brunswick, N. J., 1957.

An attractive general picture of Byzantine history and civilization. The translation includes a valuable bibliography of works dealing with all aspects of Byzantine history and civilization, compiled by Peter Charanis.

Setton, K. M. "The Byzantine Background to the Italian Renaissance," *Proceedings of the American Philosophical Society*. Volume 100, No. 1 (February, 1956). The best survey of the subject in English.

Ware, Timothy. *The Orthodox Church*. Baltimore, 1963. The best general introduction to the subject in English.

Every, George. *The Byzantine Patriarchate, 451–1204*. Second edition. London, 1962. A thoughtful and stimulating account.

Wellesz, E. *A History of Byzantine Music and Hymnography*. Second Edition. Oxford, 1961.

Wolff, H. J. *Roman Law: An Historical Introduction*. Norman, 1951.

Van der Meer, F., and C. Mohrmann. *Atlas of the Early Christian World*, translated and edited by M. F. Hedlund and H. H. Rowley. London, 1958. Maps and photographs, with annotations, illustrating the growth of the Church to the seventh century.

ARCHITECTURE AND ART:

Mathew, Gervase. *Byzantine Aesthetics*. London, 1963.

Lassus, Jean. *The Early Christian and Byzantine World*. New York, 1967.

Hamilton, J. A. *Byzantine Architecture and Decoration*. Foreword by D. Talbot Rice. Second edition. London, 1956. A convenient general account, with bibliography.

The Walters Art Gallery. *Early Christian and Byzantine Art: An Exhibition Held at the Baltimore Museum of*

Art, April 25–June 22, 1947. A notable catalogue of objects in American collections assembled for the exhibition, with excellent photographs and bibliography.

Peirce, Hayford, and Royall Tyler. *L'Art byzantin.* Vol. II. Paris, 1934. A collection of fine plates, with commentary, illustrating the art of the sixth century.

Morey, C. R. *Early Christian Art: An Outline of the Evolution of Style and Iconography in Sculpture and Painting from Antiquity to the Eighth Century.* Second edition. Princeton, 1953. A study which shows the lines of development and brings out the influence and significance of the classical tradition.

Dalton, O. M. *Byzantine Art and Archæology.* Oxford, 1911. A comprehensive survey.

Grabar, André. *L'Empereur dans l'art byzantin.* Paris, 1936. A study of the iconography and of the political and religious significance of the representations of the emperor.

–––. *Byzantine Painting: Historical and Critical Study.* Geneva, Skira, 1953.

–––. *The Art of the Byzantine Empire: Byzantine Art in the Middle Ages,* translated by Betty Forster. New York, 1966.

–––. *Byzantium: From the Death of Theodosius to the Rise of Islam,* translated by Stuart Gilbert and James Emmons. London, 1967.

Volbach, W. F. *Early Christian Art.* New York, 1962. A splendid collection of photographs, some in color, with selected architectural plans and drawings. The period through the sixth century is covered.

Beckwith, John. *The Art of Constantinople: An Introduction to Byzantine Art.* London, 1961. An excellent introductory work.

Rice, D. Talbot. *The Art of Byzantium.* London and New

York, 1959. Magnificent photographs, many in color, of the art and architecture of Constantinople, beginning with the time of Constantine the Great.

INDEX

INDEX

The seventeenth century ushered in the period of Dutch dominance in printing and typefounding. During this century, Anton Janson cut his Janson type, which is thoroughly Dutch in character. Through the years Janson has proven to be one of the most popular faces for fine bookwork in America. This book is set in ten-point Janson with two points of spacing between the lines, from a modern recutting of the classic Janson type.

UNIVERSITY OF OKLAHOMA PRESS

NORMAN